Be Nice to Me—I Pick Your Nursing Home!

How to Provide for Your Parent's Care without Going to the Poorhouse or the Nuthouse

by

Yale S. Hauptman, Esq.

Woodpecker Press, LLC
Bayville, NJ

Be Nice to Me—I Pick Your Nursing Home!
How to Provide for Your Parent's Care
without Going to the Poorhouse or the Nuthouse

Published by
Woodpecker Press, LLC
P.O. Box 316, Bayville, New Jersey 08721-0316
www.WoodpeckerPress.com
info@woodpeckerpress.com

The stories in this book are provided as examples. The names have been changed to protect the privacy of those involved. Any resemblance to actual persons, living or dead, is purely coincidental.

ISBN: 978-1-937397-03-6 (sc)
ISBN: 978-1-937397-04-3 (ebk)
ISBN: 978-1-937397-05-0 (ebk)

Printed in the United States of America
Hoboken, New Jersey

Cover design: Nu-Image Design, www.nu-imagedesign.com
On the cover: Andrew Hauptman

Dedication

*Dedicated to the memory of my grandparents
and in honor of my parents, without whom I would not be
the person I am personally and professionally.*

Personal Note from the Author

The book you are about to read is a compilation of individual articles written over a three-year period, which have appeared on my elder law blog. I have grouped the articles together in chapters by subject matter. This book can be read cover to cover, as would a novel, or it can also be used as a reference manual.

If you would like to subscribe to my blog and have posts delivered directly to your e-mail box, I urge you to go to www.hauptmanlaw.com. You'll find a link on the home page prompting you to provide your name and e-mail address, and we will immediately add you to our list.

If you live in New Jersey and would like to know more about how we can help you and your family, you can reach us by e-mail at contact@hauptmanlaw.com.

Best regards,

Yale

Table of Contents

Preface 1

Chapter 1   Introduction 3

The Difference between Elder Law and Estate Planning 3

How to Plan for the Future 5

Is the Recent Change in Social Security Policy
   a Sign of More to Come? 6

Is Medicaid Really Biased? 8

Chapter 2   Medicaid—The Rules 10

Paying for Nursing Home Care 10

Frequently Asked Questions about Medicaid 12

Medicaid Myths 14

Medicaid's Division of Assets—What Is It? 16

What Is the "DRA"? 18

Guilty until Proven Innocent: How the Medicaid System
   Differs from the Criminal System 20

Medicaid: The State's Bizarro World? 22

Hope for Haiti: Despair for Mom? 24

Spent Down? Well, Maybe Not 26

Why Good Recordkeeping is so Critical to Medicaid 28

The Relationship between Gift Taxes and Medicaid 30

Medicaid's Disabled Child Exception 32

Does an Inheritance Count for Medicaid? 34

Married—Well Not Really 35

Civil Unions and Medicaid 37

NFL Seat Licenses and Medicaid—Huh? 38

If Dad Needs Nursing Home Care,
   Will the State Take Mom's Home? 39

Chapter 3   Medicaid: The Application **41**

The Risk of Going the Medicaid Application Process Alone 41

A Medicaid Story that Starts Out Badly but Turns Out Just Fine.....43

Assisted-Living Medicaid—The Risks of "Going It Alone"...........45

Why Pay Someone to File a Medicaid Application
I Can Complete Myself?..47

Chapter 4   Medicaid—The Strategies............................**49**

Crisis Planning—Nothing Left But the House 49

The Home—To Transfer or Not to Transfer.................................51

What is a "Step Up in Basis" and Why Do I Want to Keep It? 53

How Home Ownership Can Be a Benefit in a Medicaid
Spend-Down Scenario..55

Some Married Couple Spend-Down Options to Consider...............57

How Can the Government Tell Me I Can't Help My Family? 59

How We Saved a Family $240,000 61

How a Call from Ann's Attorney Saved Her $90,000 63

Can I Be Paid to Provide Care for Mom? 64

Is My Family Business at Risk Because of Long-Term Care? 66

Dad Gets German Reparations Money—Does Mom
Get to Keep It? 68

Can I Add My Children's Names to My Bank Account
to Protect It from Medicaid? 70

Long-Term Care Insurance—How Does Medicaid View It? 72

The Right Way and the Wrong Way
to Reduce a Medicaid Penalty 74

Chapter 5   Long-Term Care Planning............................**75**

Home for the Holidays..75

The Long-Term Care Perfect Storm 77

The Team Approach to Long-Term Care Planning 78

What Families Need to Know Before a Crisis Hits 80

Is Remaining at Home Always the Best Option? 82

Long-Term Care Planning—A Real-Life Picture.............................. 83

Multigenerational Homes—A Long-Term Care
    Solution? Maybe 85

I've Got a Living Trust, So I've Got
    Long-Term Care Planning Covered 87

The Second Marriage and How It Impacts Long-Term Care 89

Retirement Accounts—Should I Take More than
    the Minimum Requirement Distribution? 91

"But Mom Won't Live to One Hundred—Or Will She?"............... 93

State Pension Crisis—How Will It Affect You? 95

If We Apply for Medicaid, Have We Given Up? 96

Chapter 6   Estate Planning..**97**

Why Do I Need a Will? 97

The Dangers of an Improperly Drafted Will 99

When Can an Alternate Executor Take Over?.............................. 101

If We Move to a New State, Do I Need a New Will?..................... 103

Living Trusts.. 104

How Long-Term Care Can Destroy an Estate Plan 106

What Michael Jackson and Yung-Ching Wang
    Can Teach Us All 108

New Estate Tax Law in 2011.. 110

I Don't Have an Estate Tax Problem—Do I? 111

Chapter 7   Estate Administration **113**

What to Do When a Loved One Dies 113

Failing to Probate in a Timely Manner... 115

How to Turn a Simple Estate Matter into a Complex Mess 117

How Harriet's Estate Plan Destroyed Her Family......................... 118

Why Edna's Estate Plan Is No Better Than Harriet's.................... 120

We Don't Owe Any Estate Tax, So What the Heck
    Is Inheritance Tax? 122

**Chapter 8   Powers of Attorney, Health-Care Directives,
          and Guardianships 124**

What Happens if My Bank Refuses to
    Honor My Power of Attorney?...124

Health-Care Directives—The Right to Make
    Medical Decisions 126

Understanding Life-Sustaining Measures....................................128

Guardianship as a Substitute for Poor Planning 130

Mom Needs Help but Won't Accept It—Can We
    Apply for Guardianship?...132

Chapter 9   Medicare...134

The Big Difference between Medicare and Medicaid 134

Obamacare—What Do Seniors Need to Know?...........................136

I'm Turning Sixty-Five—Should I Enroll in Medicare? 138

Chapter 10   VA Benefits...140

The Best Kept Secret in Long-Term Care Planning 140

Can I Get Medicaid if I Already Get VA Benefits?......................142

How VA Benefits Could Have Saved One Family.......................143

What Happens When a Veteran Dies
    While a Claim is Pending? 144

VA Extended Care Benefits...145

Chapter 11   The Effects of Alzheimer's and Dementia.................146

The Uncertainty of Alzheimer's Disease 146

One of the Clearest Warning Signs of Dementia.........................148

Early-Onset Alzheimer's 150

Alzheimer's Disease and Government Shutdowns........................152

Chapter 12   The Home 153

Saving the Home...153

Reverse Mortgages 155

A Closer Look at Reverse Mortgages 157

Chapter 13   The Nightmare Stories 158

How to Lose Medicaid 158

Is a Child Responsible for Not Pursuing Medicaid
   for a Parent? 160

Transfer of Home Leads to Medicaid Mess 161

Assisted-Living Resident with No Money and No Medicaid 162

Declining Stock Market Leads to Long-Term Care Nightmare 164

"It's Dad's Money—He Can Do What He
   Wants with It, Right?" 165

Dad Owns His Home and Needs Care 167

The Right Way and the Wrong Way to
   Hire a Home Health Aide 169

Dangers of an Unlicensed Home Health Aide 171

Why Long-Term Care is a Woman's Worst Nightmare 173

How $250,000 Went up in Smoke 175

The Second-Marriage Long-Term Care Problem 176

Laura's Dilemma—Don't Let It Be Yours 177

The Unmarried Sibling Problem 179

Jim's Grandmother Owes Medicaid $50,000—Now What? 181

"But Mom Wanted Me to Have the Money" 183

Almost Divorced and then Tragedy Strikes 185

Better to Be Ahead of the Curve 187

How to Avoid Committing Medicaid Fraud 189

"I Was Just Following the Medicaid
   Caseworker's Instructions" 191

No Money, No Penalty, No Medicaid 193

Danger of Acting on the Wrong Information 195

Tying Up Loose Ends 197

Chapter 14 Alternatives to Nursing Home Care............................**199**

Continuing Care Retirement Communities.....................................199

Dangers of Putting All Your Eggs in
One Long-Term Care Basket 201

Adult Day Care 203

Respite Care...204

Chapter 15 Long-Term Care Insurance.......................................**205**

Long-Term Care Insurance—The Basics 205

MetLife Drops Long-Term Care—What Does It
Mean for You and Me? 207

The Government's Latest Long-Term Care Solution 208

Chapter 16 Special Needs Planning **210**

Disabled Child Receives an Inheritance—Will He Lose
Government Benefits?...210

Should I Leave My Disabled Child's Inheritance
to Another to Hold?...212

Index of Essay Titles in Alphabetical Order 214

Resources 219

About the Author..220

Preface

Facing the enormity of long-term care, whether it be the financial, health-care, emotional, or psychological issues, is so overwhelming. As an elder law attorney, when I sit down with seniors and their families to explain how we can help them and guide them through that journey, we cover a lot of ground. There are so many factors and scenarios to consider. Planning for long-term care sometimes feels like trying to hit a moving target. Families rarely process it all in one sitting. It usually takes time and repetition to really understand what steps you need to take and why.

I know because I was once in their shoes—in your shoes. Nearly twenty years ago, I was a young attorney representing clients involved in motor vehicle accidents, what is known as personal injury law. I was a novice when it comes to long-term care and what was then a very new field of law called elder law. I also had the good fortune to have wonderful parents who paid for my college and law school education. Of course, this made my parents my clients for life for all legal matters, and that is how I stumbled on long-term care and the legal issues it raises.

My parents were caring, at the time, for both my grandmothers, who lived with them. When my paternal grandmother could no longer live at home, my parents were forced to move her to a nursing home. They turned to me for help getting through the daunting Medicaid process. A few years later, my maternal grandmother entered an assisted living facility, and for the next six years bounced from assisted living to hospital to nursing home and back again as her health steadily declined, until finally she, too, remained in a nursing facility.

That is how my family became my first client. I experienced the same sense of confusion and frustration that an increasing number of families suffer through every year, that my law firm and I help our clients with each and every day.

Yet, there are so many more Americans who we never reach, who don't know that there is help out there and don't know where to turn. It is for those people that I wrote this book. Many of the essays in each chapter are short real-life stories—some are what I would call success stories, and some nightmare stories. My purpose in telling them is not to provoke discussion or thought about long-term care, but to motivate you, the reader, to take action now. Providing care for an aging loved one can be one of the most trying times in anyone's life, but it can be so much easier to get through if you are prepared for it and tackle it head on.

Finally, I want to acknowledge and thank all those who have opened up to me and shared their stories. It has been a privilege to work with so many who have allowed my law firm and me to be a resource for families facing an uncertain future due to long-term care needs.

Yale S. Hauptman
August, 2011

Chapter 1

Introduction

The Difference between Elder Law and Estate Planning

When a new client comes to see us, very often the focus of attention begins with the will and estate plan.

Our clients will frequently say, "I want to make sure my assets pass to my family the way I want and that it be done with a minimum of taxes and other expenses."

Sometimes, when I meet someone and tell them that I am an elder law attorney, they invariably reply, "Oh, you do wills and trusts, right?"

So I explain the difference between elder law and estate planning, as follows: An estate plan covers the scenario of, "What happens when I die?" In the case of your assets, how will they be distributed and to whom, and can we do it minimizing estate and inheritance taxes through the use of wills and trusts.

But in today's world, increasingly, the bigger, more difficult question is, "What happens if I live?" By that I mean, what happens if I live but am not healthy and have increased health-care costs and need to rely on others for assistance, either temporarily or on a permanent basis. The estate plan does not address this need. An estate plan can help you answer the first question, but a long-term care plan can help you answer both the first and second questions.

Let's put it another way. An estate plan insures that if you have assets when you die they will be passed in the manner you wish. The key word is "if." The plan will not, however, guarantee that there will be anything left at that time to pass. Your assets could be mostly or entirely wiped out by a lengthy illness, hospital, and/or nursing home stay, leaving your spouse and other heirs with nothing. That is the dilemma in a nutshell.

So, when would you need an elder law attorney? And when would you need an estate planning attorney? If you have a level of assets sufficient to pay for long-term care under any scenario without running out of funds, then an estate planning attorney is most likely what you need. If, however, you cannot afford the $100,000 or more per year cost of nursing home care indefinitely ($200,000 or more per year in the case of a married couple), then you need an elder law attorney. In other words, can you pay that cost from your income—without dipping into your principal?

A real-life example can illustrate the dilemma. Mary and Jim live in a home valued at $400,000 and have $350,000 in additional assets. Jim is wheelchair bound and needs assistance, which to this point Mary has been providing. However, in recent months, Mary has shown signs of confusion and forgetfulness. She went to her doctor, who diagnosed her to be in the early stages of dementia.

An estate plan is important for Mary and Jim, but it won't help them deal with the problems they are now facing. How will they afford the cost of nursing home care should either or both of them need it? Who will care for Jim—and Mary—when Mary's dementia reaches a more advanced stage? Can they remain in their own home with assistance or will they need to go to a nursing home?

Mary and Jim need a life plan to meet their needs going forward, one that is tailored to their particular situation. Mary and Jim need to consult with an elder law attorney.

How to Plan for the Future

In today's ever more turbulent world, the idea of planning for the future can be daunting, but it has never been more important. But what does that mean? And is there a certain age at which it is more appropriate? The answer is that preparing a legal and financial plan is critical regardless of age or health status. There are some things to consider:

1. Update your estate plan. A good estate plan should include a durable power of attorney for health-care decisions and a living will, which is a set of instructions concerning what treatment you do or do not want in certain situations. An estate plan will also include a will and perhaps trusts, but should also include designations of beneficiaries for your assets that pass outside of your will.

2. Begin planning for retirement. It's never too early. We've all been hearing about the bleak future for Social Security, which makes it all the more important to begin planning and saving far in advance of retirement. Sitting down with a financial planner to explore investment options is a first step.

3. Consider long-term care insurance. Become educated about long-term care insurance to be able to make an informed decision as to whether or not it is right for you. Keep in mind that it may not be necessary to insure 100% of the cost of long-term care. The younger you are when you buy it, the less it will cost. Wait too long, however, and you may be too old to qualify.

4. Discuss long-term care planning with your family. So many families wait until a crisis to discuss issues of long-term care planning. Don't wait—do it now. Let your family members know your wishes (even if they are spelled out in your estate planning documents) and make sure they know where you keep your important legal and financial documents in case they need to access them in an emergency.

5. Consult with an elder law attorney. Good elder law attorneys who take a holistic approach to meeting their clients' needs will not only make sure the proper legal planning is in place, but will also refer their clients to the appropriate professionals to take care of insurance, investment, and social service needs. Consulting with an elder law attorney is always a good place to start when planning for the future.

Is the Recent Change in Social Security Policy a Sign of More to Come?

A recent decision by the Social Security Administration (SSA) to add new medical conditions to its list of "compassionate allowance" conditions, including forms of Alzheimer's disease and dementia, may signal a change in how the government views and treats those illnesses from which a disproportionate number of long-term care residents suffer. Although this change will by no means solve the growing long-term care problem in this country, it just might be the beginning of a shift in thinking—maybe.

Social Security disability and supplemental security income benefits are paid to those who have been deemed disabled and no longer able to work. The application process, however, is a complex and drawn-out one, often resulting in initial denial and then an appeal process that can take years. However, approval often opens the door to other government benefits, such as Medicaid and Medicare. A decision of disability by the SSA is proof of disability for many other state and federal programs.

The "compassionate allowance" program is Social Security's attempt to streamline the process and recognize certain conditions that clearly result in disability without extensive medical documentation, so that applicants can get much-needed benefits quickly. What is interesting is that early-onset Alzheimer's disease (Alzheimer's affecting those under age sixty-five) and mixed dementia (as in persons suffering from dementia with more than one origin, e.g., Alzheimer's and vascular dementia) appear on the most recent list of thirty-eight new conditions that the SSA deems to be so serious that it considers people with these diagnoses to "obviously meet disability standards." The complete list of 88 compassionate allowances can be found at:

http://www.socialsecurity.gov/compassionateallowances/conditions.htm

One of the problems with the long-term care system is that government benefits available to pay for care discriminate based on disease. Alzheimer's, dementia, and the like, which affect mental capabilities, are so often treated differently from diseases and illnesses, such as cancer, which are physical. Medicare, for example, provides no coverage for long-term care, which is typically needed by sufferers of Alzheimer's and dementia. This is a big reason why families so often become bankrupted by long-term care needs and why planning ahead is so critical. So, when a government agency decides to include these illnesses in its list of "fast track" diseases, it is noteworthy because it may mean these illnesses will someday be treated equally with cancer in terms of what Medicare and traditional health insurance may cover in the future. We'll need much more than that to make a dent in the problem, but you've got to start somewhere. And Social Security is as good a place as any.

Is Medicaid Really Biased?

So often, when families call in the midst of a long-term care crisis, their primary concern, they tell us, is to care for their loved one at home. For some, that will be impossible because their medical needs require nursing home care. But for others, home care is possible. Their problem, however, is Medicaid's bias toward institutional care.

What do we mean by that? First of all, when we talk about Medicaid—the primary government program that covers long-term care—we aren't talking about one single program. Medicaid actually consists of a number of different programs under the "Medicaid umbrella." All are needs-based programs, meaning there are strict financial tests, but there are some significant differences in the rules from one to the next. An important difference is that when someone meets all the eligibility requirements for institutional Medicaid (care administered in a nursing home or state institution), the state must cover the applicant's care costs.

That is not true for home-based and other community Medicaid programs. Most states limit the number of residents for whom those benefits will be provided, resulting in lengthy waiting lists. If you have spent all your money in order to qualify for Medicaid at home, you could still wind up on a waiting list. And if you can't wait because your health is at risk, then your only alternative is to go to a nursing home. That is how the system drives people to institutional care.

In recent years, there has been increasing discussion about whether this bias is what the government really wants. Isn't it less expensive to administer care at home, which would then cost the state less money? That is a debate that you'll hear more of as the federal and state governments struggle with budget deficits and with trying to keep costs down. We have already seen, in the past five to ten years, an increase in state spending on home- and community-based programs. But some lawmakers fear what they call the "woodwork effect." If they expand these programs, giving people what they want, more will be encouraged to apply, and the costs will thus rise. People will be "coming out of the woodwork," so to speak. (Makes you wonder how much the government really cares.)

That premise is debatable. A 2009 University of California study found that expanding home-based care programs saved states money in the long run. There were additional "start up" costs for these new programs, but over time the additional expense paid for itself because, the study found, the cost of home care is cheaper than institutional care.

As we see 77 million baby boomers starting to turn sixty-five, the discussion will only intensify. The long-term care problem isn't going away.

Chapter 2

Medicaid—The Rules

Paying for Nursing Home Care

Paying for nursing home care is a huge concern for many people today. Not everyone has a long-term care insurance policy, nor do they have enough funds to privately pay for their care.

In a nursing home situation, Medicare might pay for skilled nursing care, but only for a short period of time. Most people in a nursing home are receiving custodial care. Medicare does not cover custodial care. That is when the Medicaid program becomes necessary.

What is Medicaid? Medicaid is a benefits program that is cofunded by the federal and state governments and administered by each state. The basic rules of the program are determined by federal law, but many other rules are left to the states to determine. For this reason, Medicaid programs vary, in many respects, from state to state.

The Medicaid program will pay for long-term care in a nursing home once you've qualified. That stay may be caused by Alzheimer's or Parkinson's disease, illnesses for which there is no known cure. The patient needs help with what we call the activities of daily living—eating, dressing, bathing, walking, and toileting. This is what we call "custodial care." Medicare does not pay for custodial care. In that instance, you'll either have to pay privately (i.e., use long-term care insurance or your own funds), or you'll have to qualify for Medicaid.

Why seek advice for Medicaid? As life expectancies and long-term care costs continue to rise, the challenge quickly becomes one of how to pay for these services. Many people cannot afford to pay $8,500 to $10,000 per month or more for the cost of a nursing home, and those who can pay for a while may find their life savings wiped out in a matter of months—rather than years.

Fortunately, the Medicaid program is there to help. In fact, in our lifetime, Medicaid has become the long-term care insurance of the middle class. But the eligibility to receive Medicaid benefits requires that you pass certain tests on the amount of income and assets that you have. The reason for Medicaid planning is simple. First, you need to provide enough assets for the security of your loved ones—they too may have a similar crisis. Second, the rules are extremely complicated and confusing. The result is that without planning and advice, many people spend more than they should and their family security is jeopardized.

> ***Elder Care Point:*** *Many people cannot afford to pay $8,500 to $10,000 per month or more for the cost of a nursing home, and those who can pay for a while may find their life savings wiped out in a matter of months.*

Frequently Asked Questions about Medicaid

Q: Once I qualify for Medicaid, will the quality of care I receive be substandard?

A: No. It is illegal for a facility to discriminate against Medicaid recipients. By law, Medicaid patients must receive the same level of care as private-pay residents.

Q: Is a married couple always required to spend down half of their assets before qualifying for Medicaid?

A: Not always. In fact, oftentimes couples have over $100,000 and qualify for Medicaid benefits without spending a penny. Although couples must meet income and asset criteria before one of them qualifies for benefits, federal and state laws were written to protect individuals from becoming impoverished if their spouse needs nursing home care. Medicaid planning is like tax planning. Legislation has provided legal exceptions to the general rules, which, with good advice from a knowledgeable professional, can save families thousands of dollars.

Q: Is it true that under current Medicaid laws a parent cannot make financial gifts to their children once they have entered the nursing home?

A: No. In fact, a proper gifting program can be part of a Medicaid planning technique. At the time an applicant applies for Medicaid, the state will "look back" five years to see if any gifts have been made. Any financial gifts or transfers for less than fair market value during the five-year look back may cause a delay in an applicant's eligibility. A proper gifting program requires calculating the penalties before making gifts.

Q: Can't I make gifts of $13,000 per year and still get Medicaid benefits?

A: No. The $13,000 per year gift people ask about when discussing Medicaid is a gift tax exclusion number. That same gift, however, could very well cause a Medicaid penalty or waiting period for benefits. Medicaid rules say we take the amount of the transfer and divide by the monthly average cost of nursing home care. Some states use one statewide average. A minority of states (New York is an example) break up the state into regions, and use a different number for each region. The resulting number is the "penalty." Although a $13,000 gift will not cause you to pay gift taxes on it (from a tax-law perspective), it may cause a Medicaid transfer penalty.

Q: A Medicaid applicant's house is considered "exempt" under Medicaid laws. Can an applicant give their house away without incurring penalties?

A: Probably not. Any assets that are given away (personal property or real property) are considered gifts. (Medicaid's term is "transfer for less than fair value.") If an applicant gives his house away, the state will assess a penalty, a period of ineligibility, based on the fair market value of the house at the time it was transferred. There are certain transfers that are exempt from the transfer rules. A qualified elder law attorney can review with you whether any of these exceptions apply to you and your family.

Q: Once my spouse is approved for Medicaid, can I gift my assets away?

A: It depends on your state's laws. Once the "institutionalized" spouse has been approved for Medicaid, the "community" spouse's assets are no longer a part of the ongoing continuing eligibility for the "Medicaid" spouse. This is called "division of assets." A transfer of assets by the community spouse after the division of assets occurs would cause a Medicaid transfer penalty for the community spouse, but not the Medicaid spouse, although some states challenge this because the rules are a bit ambiguous.

There are a number of steps a Medicaid applicant can take to preserve their assets, including gifting strategies, personal care contracts, raising the community spouse resource allowance, etc. What you need to remember is that the laws are constantly changing, and the planning your neighbor did for their mother six months ago may not be proper for your mother tomorrow.

Medicaid Myths

Medicaid was considered a complicated program when President Lyndon B. Johnson first signed it into law in 1965, and it has grown more complex each year. Although it is a national program, it is administered by each state. The rules and regulations are constantly changing, and can vary widely from state to state. So, it's no wonder there are many myths and inaccuracies surrounding the program.

Let's take a look at some of the common misconceptions we hear frequently about Medicaid.

"My mother heard about someone who..."

All too often, we meet people who have heard horror stories about Medicaid from well-meaning friends or family, filled with inaccuracies and half-truths that frighten people into spending every last dime on nursing home care before turning to Medicaid for help.

Similar stories have also prompted people to assume that what worked for a friend will work for them as well. So, they may give their house or all of their assets to a child in hopes that impoverishing themselves will immediately qualify them for benefits. Unfortunately, they soon find out that these transfers mean they are unable to receive benefits for months or even years after the money is gone.

"My father is already in the nursing home, so there's nothing we can do now."

It's true that families often wait longer than they should to plan for long-term care, but that doesn't necessarily mean it's too late to establish a good plan. A good rule of thumb is that the earlier a plan is begun, the more assets can be preserved, especially with the most recent Medicaid changes that extended the look-back time to five years and delayed the start date of the Medicaid ineligibility period.

So, when is the right time to plan? If you are in your sixties and in good health, now is the time. Ideally, you want to put a plan in place while you are still healthy to ensure maximum asset protection. That includes having a power of attorney in place for financial and health-care decisions—before a gradual or sudden decline in mental competency occurs. It's also important to make sure the durable power of attorney contains the right language so Medicaid planning is possible.

You should immediately begin planning if you think that nursing home care will be needed by a loved one. This may be due to a diagnosis of a terminal or debilitating illness, such as Alzheimer's, Parkinson's, or ALS. These situations should be reviewed by an elder law attorney to determine the type of planning to be done.

"The Medicaid office can just give me the paperwork."

Those who work in the Medicaid office cannot offer you legal advice. You may not learn about laws that may allow you to receive Medicaid and still keep part or all of your spouse's income as well as your own. Nor can they represent you or give you advice on the laws that, depending on your specific situation, may allow you to keep all of your assets without spending down a single penny. Medicaid has rules and regulations in place to ensure families don't lose everything to nursing home costs. An elder law attorney can explain how those laws may benefit you and your family.

"Our prenuptial agreement shows that everything belongs to my husband."

We hear this often in cases of second marriages. The state generally does not take prenuptial agreements into consideration when determining Medicaid eligibility. All assets owned by either spouse are considered jointly owned and must be divided and spent down exactly as they would if there was no prenuptial agreement in place. The only way a prenuptial agreement is effective is if the couple actually divorces.

Proper estate planning and expert legal advice can ensure that the wishes of both spouses are honored regardless of which one needs nursing home care. The bottom line is that the new changes have made Medicaid planning more difficult—but not impossible. Individuals who plan early, while still healthy and years before nursing home care is needed, will be in the best position to preserve their hard-earned assets and maintain control of their financial affairs. Consult with an elder law attorney, who can help you navigate through the maze of rules.

Medicaid's Division of Assets—What is it?

Division of assets is the name commonly used for the method by which Medicaid attempts to protect the healthy spouse from becoming impoverished when the ill spouse needs to spend down in order to qualify for Medicaid. It applies only to married couples. The law intended to change the eligibility requirements for Medicaid in situations where one spouse needs nursing home care while the other spouse remains in the community (i.e., at home or in an assisted-living facility). The law, in effect, recognizes that it makes little sense to impoverish both spouses when only one needs to qualify for Medicaid assistance for nursing home care.

As a result of this recognition, division of assets was born. Basically, in a division of assets, the couple gathers all of their nonexempt (countable) assets together in a review. See box on the next page for a list of exempt assets.

The nonexempt assets are then divided in two, with the community (or at-home) spouse allowed to keep half of all countable assets up to a maximum of $109,540. The other half of the countable assets must be "spent down" until $2,000 remains. The amount of countable assets that the at-home spouse gets to keep is called the community spouse resource allowance (CSRA).

The maximum CSRA is $109,540 and the minimum is $21,912, meaning the community spouse gets to keep at least that amount, even if the couple does not have $43,824 ($21,912 × 2). Some states don't use the minimum, so the community spouse keeps the first $109,540, regardless of the total asset level. Also be aware that these numbers are adjusted for inflation each year; so, it is best to consult with a knowledgeable elder law attorney in your state.

Recognizing that assets fluctuate in value from month to month or day to day because of market conditions and spending, at what point in time does the state value the assets, or take its "snapshot of the assets?" The snapshot is taken as of the first day of the first month of continuous institutionalization. A stay in an acute-care hospital is generally not considered institutionalized. Residing in a Medicaid-certified nursing home, psychiatric hospital, or licensed special hospital is generally considered to be institutionalization under the regulations.

Because of the timing of the snapshot, opportunities often exist to maximize the amount the community spouse can keep under the CSRA, especially when institutionalization is anticipated because of rapidly declining health.

Assets Considered Exempt

- The home, no matter its value. The home must be the principal place of residence.

- Household and personal belongings, furniture, appliances, jewelry, and clothing.

- One vehicle, but there may be some limitations on value.

- Burial plot and irrevocable funeral plans for you and your spouse. There may be some limitations on the plans themselves.

- Cash value life insurance policies, as long as the face amount of all policies combined does not exceed $1,500. If they do exceed $1,500, then the cash value in these policies is countable.

- Cash and other assets, not more than $2,000.

Elder Care Point: The law, in effect, recognizes that it makes little sense to impoverish both spouses when only one needs to qualify for Medicaid assistance for nursing home care.

What is the "DRA"?

On February 1, 2006, the House of Representatives passed the 776-page Deficit Reduction Act of 2005 (DRA), which includes substantial Medicaid changes. President Bush signed the legislation on February 8, 2006, making the changes the law of the land. So, what exactly are these changes?

The first is that the Medicaid gifting or asset transfer rules have been changed so that the "look-back" period for all asset transfers is now five years. This includes any transfers made on or after February 8, 2006. Under the old rules, transfers that did not involve a trust resulted in asset transfer penalties of no more than three years. Now, under the new legislation, all asset transfers will have a look-back period of five years.

In addition, the start of the penalty period won't begin until the Medicaid applicant is already spent down. For instance, under the old rules a gift of $65,000 would create a ten-month penalty (this penalty varies from state to state and is adjusted periodically) from the date of the gift.

Under the new law, that period of ineligibility will not begin until the gift has been made and the spend down has been completed. Only then will the penalty period begin, meaning that the gifted funds may have to be given back to pay for care. You can imagine the nightmares this might cause for unsuspecting nursing home residents and their families.

In addition, the new law makes any individual with home equity of more than $500,000 (or if the states elect, they can raise this to $750,000) ineligible for Medicaid. In other words, under the old law the home was an exempt asset. Under the new law the home may be an exempt asset, but only so long as the home equity is not greater than $500,000 (or $750,000). This limitation does not apply if the spouse continues to live in the home.

The new law changes the annuity rules. Annuities will be treated differently under the new law. In addition, the law will require the state to be named as the remainder beneficiary on annuities.

Partial penalties are no longer rounded down. Under the old law, if a transfer resulted in a partial month penalty, that number was rounded down to the lower whole number. Now, all fractions are counted. This is significant where penalties of less than one month result. Previously, they carried no penalty. Now they do.

The bottom line is that the new law greatly complicates the Medicaid application process. Individuals may find that inadvertent transfers may prevent them from qualifying for Medicaid. The advice of an experienced elder law attorney has become more important than ever under these new rules.

Guilty until Proven Innocent: How the Medicaid System Differs from the Criminal System

"Mom and Dad have always been big believers in paying cash for everything. They don't use credit cards," John tells me.

"Don't buy on credit," they always said. Although that's a pretty sound financial approach, it can get Mom and Dad into hot water when it comes time to apply for Medicaid. That's because the Medicaid system works very differently from the criminal system. Let me explain.

First of all, you need to understand some basics about how Medicaid works. In order to qualify, one must spend down assets first. When essentially all your money is gone (in the case of a married couple the healthy spouse gets to keep a small amount), then Medicaid will kick in. However, if you have made transfers for less than fair value, what most people would call gifts, then you won't be eligible for Medicaid. The greater those transfers are, the longer your ineligibility period will be.

And before the government will step in and pay for your care, it will insist that you show how you spent your money. And by "show," I mean on paper, by producing each and every financial statement dating back five years from the date you apply for benefits. So, this is where my reference to the criminal system comes in. Everyone knows from grade school the concept of "innocent until proven guilty." With Medicaid, however, that concept is turned around. You are "guilty" until proven "innocent" when it comes to transfers for less than fair value. By that, I mean to say, if you can't prove what you have spent your money on, then Medicaid will consider it a transfer for less than fair value, a "gift" in essence, causing a denial of benefits.

Let's now go back to John's parents. As we know, cash is hard to trace. Think about it. If Mom and Dad have been withdrawing cash for their spending needs, how hard is it going to be to prove, going back as many as five years, what they spent that money on? All we'll see on their bank statements are cash withdrawals. No explanations. Who keeps all those receipts? Hardly anyone. But that's what Mom and Dad must do in order to preserve their eligibility for government benefits.

So, how do they avoid this potentially catastrophic result? They must better prepare themselves for the possibility of needing long-term care—well before they need it—and consulting with a knowledgeable elder law attorney, who can tell them how to spend down their assets and establish a clear paper trail while preserving their ability to qualify for government benefits, would be a wise move.

> **Elder Care Point:** *With Medicaid...You are "guilty" until proven "innocent" when it comes to transfers for less than fair value... if you can't prove what you have spent your money on, then Medicaid will consider it a transfer for less than fair value, a "gift" in essence, causing a denial of benefits.*

Medicaid: The State's Bizarro World?

You may be a fan of Superman or, like me, Seinfeld, and in that case, are familiar with the term "bizarro" The term is part of popular culture. *Wikipedia's* definition of bizarro is *a weirdly mutilated version of anything.* I am fond of telling clients that entering the "Medicaid world" means one must throw out logic and lifelong habits, which can get you in trouble when attempting to obtain Medicaid benefits. I explain to our clients that much of what we tell them to do is necessarily counterintuitive to what they have done their whole lives because they are entering the bizarro world of Medicaid. Allow me to explain.

I had a conversation last week with a married couple for whom we are preparing a Medicaid application. John is in a nursing home, and Mary is healthy and living at home. I explained to them that Mary can keep half of their countable assets, in their case $75,000, but that they must spend down to below that dollar amount by the last day of the month directly preceding the month we want to qualify John for Medicaid.

I have had this conversation numerous times with clients in John and Mary's situation, and know all too well that this simple instruction is not always followed. The largest part of most spend downs typically goes to the nursing home. But, as most people do, myself included, we wait until we get a bill before we pay it. If I owe you money, I'm not going to chase after you for a bill. Whenever you get around to it and invoice me, then I'll pay it. The longer the money stays in my bank account, the happier I am.

However, this can get you into big trouble and cost you tens of thousands of dollars if you wait for the nursing home bill. If we want John to be eligible for Medicaid next month and we know that he owes the nursing home $20,000 for the past two months of care, but the nursing home hasn't yet presented Mary with a bill, it does not matter that Mary and John legitimately owe the facility the money. If that $20,000 is still sitting in their bank account next month, causing their account balance to exceed $75,000, John cannot qualify for Medicaid. Even worse than that, he can't even qualify for next month. He has to wait until the following month, which means they will owe the facility another $10,000, leaving Mary with $65,000 to live on.

That is why we are so focused on getting our clients to change their habits, which isn't easy to do. Their entire lives John and Mary have paid their bills—after the vendor presents them with an invoice. However, I tell them they must get the nursing home to bill them ASAP. Who chases after someone to whom they owe tens of thousands of dollars? However, that's the way it goes in the bizarro world of Medicaid—and why entering this strange land without a knowledgeable guide can literally cost you tens of thousands of dollars.

> **Elder Care Point:** *Entering the "Medicaid world" means one must throw out logic and lifelong habits, which can get you in trouble when attempting to obtain Medicaid benefits.*

Hope for Haiti: Despair for Mom?

The recent outpouring of support for the victims of the earthquakes in Haiti and Japan highlight a question often asked about gifting and charitable contributions as it relates to Medicaid. For example, last week Diane called me to ask whether it is okay for Mom to make a charitable contribution to help the earthquake relief effort. You would think that helping out others in need is a good thing, something to be encouraged. Well, the answer is not so clear cut when it comes to Medicaid eligibility.

Diane's mom is now living in a nursing facility and is in spend-down mode. In her case, she will be eligible for Medicaid in three years if she lives that long. But to preserve her right to benefits, she must do more than spend down her remaining assets. She must spend in such a way that she receives something of equal monetary value in return. Now, she'll spend most of it on her nursing care but what about charitable contributions? Does Diane's mom receive fair value back for the contribution? Or does she make a transfer for less than fair value, which will then result in a Medicaid penalty—a period of ineligibility, which, by the way, doesn't start until she has no more money left?

Certainly, Mom is getting a benefit. She is helping others in need, but that is not exactly something we can put a monetary value on. The same answer would seem to be the case for contributions to Mom's favorite religious or civic charities. But what if she makes a small gift of, say, $100? Will that cause a penalty?

Applying the Medicaid rule as written, any transfer for less than fair value, no matter how small, will trigger a penalty. And think about it. If the state goes through five years of your financial records (that's the five-year look back), how many of these charitable contributions and other transfers might it find? If we total them up, it might turn out to be a pretty big number, causing a few months or more of ineligibility. And don't you think that if the state can delay paying for Mom's nursing home care, at a time when many state governments are financially strapped, it would do so?

On the other hand, if Mom's charitable contributions are small, infrequent, and far enough in advance of her application for Medicaid, they most likely won't cause a problem. But that's what makes the whole long-term care system so frustrating. It's the uncertainty, not knowing what you can or can't do. That's why it is so important to seek advice from a trusted advisor first. You just don't want to take the wrong step. In Diane's case, I told her a small gift would be OK. It didn't make me feel good having to tell her that the government laws and rules in this case discourage charitable giving. But that's a whole separate discussion for another time.

Spent Down? Well, Maybe Not

The ins and outs of Medicaid are complex and confusing. Another example that we recently addressed in our office highlights that point. Mr. Jones lived in a nursing home, and we prepared an application for institutional Medicaid. Under Medicaid rules, the applicant needs to be below $2,000 in assets as of the first moment of the first day of the month in order to qualify for Medicaid for that month. We tell clients that they must be below this number as of the last day of the preceding month.

Spending down means making transfers for value, that is to say, a purchase of goods or services for equal value. Very often, this spend down occurs right up until the last day of the month. So, what happens if I write a check to pay a bill on the thirty-first of the month but the person or business I give it to doesn't cash it until the next month? As long as it is dated the thirty-first (or earlier) and you give it to that person or business no later than the thirty-first, then it is counted as being spent, even though it will not clear your checking account until the next month.

Now, this all sounds very trivial, and I would agree with you, but don't think for a minute that the state will overlook these transactions. They won't. They scrutinize each one very carefully. If you're over the Medicaid limit by a dollar, you're over for that month and have to wait until the next month.

Let's go back to Mr. Jones. His son, Bill, was spending down Dad's assets. He had credit card, rent, and utility bills to pay. We spoke on the thirty-first and Bill confirmed that Dad's three accounts totaled $1,200 after accounting for payments. Now, we didn't have statements yet for one of the accounts, so we had to rely on Bill's word. We filed the application, and several weeks passed before we heard from the Medicaid office. They wanted missing statements from one of the accounts at an out-of-state bank. We obtained those statements but were surprised to learn that some of the bills were not paid by check, but rather by electronic transfer—on the first of the month. So, while Bill kept telling us that Dad's accounts totaled $1,200, that was not, in fact, true. He was counting these electronic debits, but Medicaid would not.

As it turned out, we still were under $2,000 in Mr. Jones' case, but not by much. (We tell clients we want them to be well below $2,000 to leave room for just these types of surprises.) The next case may not work out so favorably. Just another example of how tricky the Medicaid rules really are and why you don't want to go it alone.

Why Good Recordkeeping is so Critical to Medicaid

Over time, the Medicaid changes contained in the Deficit Reduction Act of 2005 will have harsh and far-reaching effects on the average American who needs nursing home care. Let's review some of those changes.

1. Start date of the Medicaid Penalty. The penalty for transfers no longer starts when the transfer is made, but rather when all other assets have been spent down, the individual needs nursing home–level care, and he/she applies for Medicaid. In that way, the state can be sure it will impose the penalty at exactly the time when Medicaid is needed.

2. Penalties can no longer be rounded down. The penalty (period of Medicaid ineligibility) is determined by dividing the amount transferred by the average monthly cost of nursing home care (determined by each state). Under the old law, that number was rounded down. In other words, fractional amounts were not considered. The new law says that fractional amounts must now be considered. The impact of this change can be illustrated as follows. If I transfer $3,500 and the average cost of nursing home care in my state is $7,000, the penalty is now a half month, whereas previously there was no penalty. In fact, a transfer of as little as $210 will cause a one-day penalty.

3. All transfers are added together and treated as one transfer when calculating the Medicaid penalty. Medicaid will look back five years from the date of the Medicaid application for transfers, add them together, and assess one penalty as if the transfers were made in one lump sum.

4. The Medicaid look back is extended to five years. This means that together with the Medicaid application, one must provide five years of financial records, which Medicaid will carefully review to determine if there are any Medicaid disqualifying transfers.

The implications of these changes are readily apparent. No matter how small, all gifts, cash withdrawals, checks payable to cash, payments to family members who may have laid out funds to cover expenses, payments for grandchildren's college tuition, and cash payments to home health aides, house cleaning, etc., will be challenged by Medicaid. It is irrelevant that when these transactions occurred Medicaid and nursing home care were not even a thought in anyone's mind. Any transfers that cannot be explained, (i.e., documentation produced to show they were not subject to a transfer penalty) will cause Medicaid ineligibility.

So, what should you do? Take steps now to get your financial records in order. Learn how to avoid these Medicaid traps. Very often, by catching these problems early, you can fix them.

The Relationship between Gift Taxes and Medicaid

Joe calls me because he wants to understand how Medicaid works. I start to explain how you have to spend down your assets before you can qualify for benefits. That the spend down has to be for value, meaning that you are spending your money and receiving something of equal value in product or service in return. Joe listens and then perks up.

"Wait a second," he says. I can make a gift of $10,000 per person, so that doesn't count, right?"

"Wrong," I replied. "You're confusing the annual gift tax exclusion with the Medicaid rules.

What Joe has done is make a very common mistake. So let's run through the basics and clear it up. Gift tax is paid when you make a sizable gift to someone who isn't your spouse. One of the purposes of the gift tax law is to protect the estate tax. For example, if I know that my estate will be taxed when I die, then why don't I just transfer all my assets to my loved ones shortly before I die? The gift tax eliminates this estate tax avoidance strategy.

A certain amount, however, is exempt from the gift tax. For 2011 and 2012, there is a lifetime exclusion of $5,000,000, meaning I can transfer up to that amount, in one lump sum or in smaller increments, over my lifetime. In addition, I can gift up to $13,000 per person per year (everyone remembers it as $10,000, but several years back an inflation adjustment was added, so the number now is $13,000). So, there is no gift tax owed when you make that gift, but it does carry a Medicaid transfer penalty.

How so? Because the gift tax rules have nothing to do with the Medicaid rules. On the one hand, the government is telling us it's OK to gift some amount of money without paying tax, but only up to a point. On the other hand, if we need nursing home care, the government doesn't want to pay for that care unless we spend all of our own money on that care first.

Every $13,000 gift, therefore, carries a Medicaid transfer penalty, a period during which you are not eligible for Medicaid. That penalty, expressed in months, is calculated by taking the transfer for less than fair value (the gift, as we have been discussing) and dividing by the average monthly cost of nursing home care. This number is set by each state, and in some states it varies by region. If that number is $6,500, this means every $13,000 tax-free gift carries a Medicaid penalty of two months.

Now, does that mean that you should never make gifts? No, not necessarily. It just means that in today's increasingly complicated world, you have to understand that making those gifts can result in long-term consequences, which you may not recognize until it's too late. That's why a carefully thought-out long-term care plan is critical, and getting the proper guidance well before that care is needed is always the best approach.

Medicaid's Disabled Child Exception

How many times have you contacted a government office to inquire about some benefit or program only to be told you are not eligible? Have you then left the office or hung up the phone accepting that to be true? What if it's just flat out wrong? As an elder law attorney, I see that happen all the time—especially when it comes to the Medicaid program. A recent court case corrected at least one of those untruths.

A federal court finally weighed in on a particular exception to the Medicaid transfer rules that the State of New Jersey has, for some time, misinterpreted. A transfer of assets from parent to child, if made within five years of the date of application for Medicaid benefits, carries a Medicaid penalty, but there are some exceptions to that general rule. If the transfer is made to a disabled child, or to a trust for the benefit of a disabled child, then that transfer is not subject to a Medicaid penalty. The state has, for as long as I can remember, insisted that this exception applies only if the transfer is to a trust for the sole benefit of the disabled child.

Now, if you are not familiar with the ins and outs of the Medicaid laws and were told that your mother is ineligible for this reason, what would you do? Probably go home and wait until the Medicaid penalty expires, not knowing any better. When this sort of thing happens in our office, we first go back to the federal law and state regulations to show the state caseworker the error of his/her ways. Sometimes that is enough to resolve the issue, but other times the state doesn't budge and we, as elder law attorneys, have to resort to the court system to settle the dispute. In the case I am referring to, the issue came down, in part, to the type of grammar lesson you might remember from elementary school about the proper placement of a comma. The state's interpretation didn't seem logical, and the court agreed.

One of my staff members asked me why the state would take a position that seems so farfetched. The answer, I think, can be found by looking at the bigger picture of what is playing out in this country. The government doesn't have enough money to fund the programs and services it currently has. Looking at what's coming, the number of people facing a long-term–care crisis will continue to increase in the next twenty years as 77 million baby boomers reach senior status. So, you can expect the state to continue to interpret eligibility standards very strictly. And sometimes they'll get it completely wrong. That's why the do-it-yourself approach is dangerous. You could be losing valuable benefits, and without the assistance of someone with knowledge of the laws, you wouldn't even know it. The government wants to push you to the back of the line. Make sure you protect yourself and fight to maintain your spot at the front.

Does an Inheritance Count for Medicaid?

Timing is everything—a well-worn cliché, but also so very true of life in general. It's certainly true in Medicaid planning when it comes to receiving an inheritance. Let's take a look.

Does an inheritance count as an asset for Medicaid purposes? For a single person, the answer is clearly, "Yes." If a single individual is spending down his or her assets, and before the spend down is completed, that individual receives an inheritance, then those assets are added to whatever that person has and must be spent down to $2,000 before eligibility will be completed. Likewise, if that person has already qualified for Medicaid, and then receives an inheritance, that inheritance must also be spent down before eligibility is again established. (It may be easier in some instances to simply give the inheritance to the state and remain on Medicaid.)

What about the case of an inheritance received by the community spouse where the other spouse is in a nursing home? This is the situation where timing is everything.

In the case of a married couple, if the at-home, or community spouse, receives an inheritance before the nursing home spouse is eligible for Medicaid, then those inherited assets are countable for Medicaid purposes.

If, on the other hand, the community spouse receives an inheritance (or, for that matter, a gift) after the nursing home spouse is eligible for Medicaid, then there is no impact on the eligibility of the nursing home spouse. Regulations clearly provide that the community spouse may acquire property after the nursing home spouse is eligible without affecting the status of the community spouse. For that reason, the timing of when property is acquired can be crucial. Although it may not always be possible to affect the timing of the receipt of an inheritance or a gift, where possible, if the community spouse can hold off until after Medicaid qualification, then these newly acquired funds would belong to the community spouse absolutely and would not be a countable resource of the nursing home spouse.

If you're thinking about not accepting the inheritance by executing a disclaimer, a legal refusal to take the inheritance, in most states Medicaid will treat the disclaimer as a transfer for less than fair value subject to an ineligibility (or penalty) period, so be careful.

Married—Well Not Really

Jane calls me to relate the same problem that many Americans today are coping with—trying to care for aging parents. She calls because Dad's health is rapidly deteriorating and she fears he will need nursing home care. I ask about Mom's health. Jane replies that she is healthy. And here is the twist, where the story becomes more complicated.

Jane tells me that Mom and Dad have been separated for years. Never divorced, just living separate lives under separate roofs, with separate assets.

"Dad was never easy to live with," she tells me, "but Mom wasn't the type to file for divorce. It wasn't acceptable."

"So," she asks me, "we can spend down Dad's assets and then qualify him for Medicaid, right?"

"Well," I tell her, "it's a bit more complicated than that." Under Medicaid rules, because they are still married, all their assets are combined for purposes of calculating how much to spend down. Medicaid rules do provide that if the applicant is separated from a spouse for at least one month, then he will be treated as a single person and only his assets will count toward the asset spend down. However, there is no definition of what constitutes a separation, and you can be sure that the state will scrutinize it very closely. Mom may still have to spend some of her assets for Dad's care even though they have been living single lives for years.

"Is there anything we can do," Jane asks, as I hear the desperation in her voice.

Divorce is still an option, although it could be considerably more difficult if Dad doesn't have the mental capacity to understand the legal process and consent to a divorce settlement. There is also the matter of the state, again, scrutinizing the divorce, especially if Mom has accumulated, and wants to keep, more than 50% of the combined assets. You see, the state assumes the divorce was obtained for the purpose of qualifying for Medicaid. If Mom keeps more than half the assets, Dad would probably be turned down for benefits. There may also be other strategies for married couples that could be employed to preserve assets for Mom but, although they are married under the law, they are not really "together." So, preserving Dad's assets for Mom and vice versa is not the goal.

As Jane puts it, "Mom and Dad have lived separate lives for many years. Mom has struggled to accumulate her own assets and become self-sufficient. How can I tell her that she will lose some of her hard-earned money?"

I didn't have an answer for Jane. I do, however, have one for others who may one day be in that situation. If any of Jane's story sounds familiar to you, don't wait until long-term care is staring you in the face. Plan ahead and solve the problem before it reaches crisis proportions or you'll be faced with the dilemma that Jane and her family now must tackle.

Civil Unions and Medicaid

The past few years have seen failed attempts by supporters of same-sex marriage to expand the definition of marriage to include gay and lesbian unions. However, some states have passed laws creating domestic partnerships and civil unions, which then carry with them some of the benefits of marriage. New Jersey, for example, has a civil union law that was established in 2007. So, how would partners in a civil union be treated for Medicaid purposes? Not surprisingly, the answer isn't so clear cut.

Although Medicare is a federal program governed by rules established by Congress, Medicaid, on the other hand, is a mix of federal and state law. It's that attempted blend of two governmental systems and sets of laws and regulations that makes the Medicaid system so uncertain for those trying to tap into it. The issue of civil unions is a perfect example.

New Jersey's law states that civil union couples are entitled to the same benefits (as well as held to the same set of responsibilities) as heterosexual spouses, including Medicaid. But, it's not that simple. Of course, with the government it never is. That's because there is a certain federal law known as the Defense of Marriage Act, which says that in interpreting any act of Congress, the term marriage means only a legal union between a man and a woman. This presents a problem for states recognizing civil unions because they get federal money to support their Medicaid programs. So, they may be violating federal law and could lose federal funding by treating civil union partners as married for Medicaid purposes. At least that's what the federal agency overseeing Medicare and Medicaid has indicated on at least one occasion. On the other hand, New Jersey's civil union law seems quite clear that civil union couples are to be treated as married for purposes of Medicaid.

Where does that leave things? We'll probably have to battle this one out in court. And, by the way, it isn't necessarily the case that treating civil union partners as married is best when it comes to Medicaid. Each case must be examined individually. In some instances it would be advantageous to be married; in others it wouldn't. But, the question does raise some interesting issues and is just another example of why the long-term care system is so impossibly confusing to navigate alone.

NFL Seat Licenses and Medicaid—Huh?

I met with Dave's family, who presented the following scenario. Dad needed nursing home care and the family had done no long-term planning. We talked about how under Medicaid rules the couple's assets would be counted and divided in half, and that Mom would be able to keep the home and 50% of the assets up to a maximum of $109,540. We went through a list of their investments. I then asked if they had anything else of value. Son, Dave, mentioned that Dad had just signed up for Jets season tickets at their new stadium.

"We want to keep the tickets in the family," he said. "Dad can just transfer them to us, right?"

That got me thinking. "I'm not so sure," I replied.

If you're a sports fan, you know all about seat licenses. Most NFL teams are selling season tickets in a new way. Before you can have the privilege of buying a game ticket, you must pay a fee, called a seat license. The better the seat, the higher the fee. Dave told me that the license for his family's seats cost Dad $60,000. So, what do you think will happen if Dad just transfers his seats and later applies for Medicaid?

Certainly there is no mention of NFL seat licenses in any state Medicaid regulations. But, doesn't the license have a value? Teams are telling their fans that they can resell the license—that it's really an investment. It isn't a stretch, then, for the state to treat the transfer of the license from one generation to another as a transfer for less than fair value, subject to a Medicaid penalty. Especially since the state is facing huge budget deficits and can ill afford to pay out benefits to huge numbers of its residents. So, do I think that the state will let it go? Not likely.

Back to Dave and his parents. I told him that any transfer of the seat license had to be for fair value. But, that's easier said than done. No one really knows what resale value they have since both Jet and Giant seat licenses (they share a newly built stadium) are brand new and can't even be resold yet. There is a lesson to be learned though. Families with season ticket plans may want to consider transferring them to the next generation while healthy. Just another reason it's a good idea to plan for long-term care, and if you're a Jet fan like me, you don't want to miss out on the possibility of a Super Bowl trip, which would be our first since 1969. It's gotta happen one of these years—right?

If Dad Needs Nursing Home Care, Will the State Take Mom's Home?

It's a question I get—or some variation of it—probably more often than any other, and it refers to what is called "estate recovery." As part of the deal that the states enter into with the federal government before they can get federal funding for their Medicaid programs, each state has to make an effort to recoup the money it paid out in benefits after the Medicaid recipient dies.

The process by which this is done is called estate recovery, and as with most things Medicaid, that process differs greatly from state to state. First, let's review the basics. In my state, New Jersey, estate recovery applies only to Medicaid benefits provided for services received after age fifty-five. The state will not seek immediate recovery as long as there is a surviving spouse or child under age twenty-one, blind, or permanently and totally disabled. The key word is "immediate." After the spouse and/or child dies, reaches age twenty-one, or is no longer disabled, as the case may be, the state will then attempt to recover assets from the deceased Medicaid beneficiary's estate.

A common misconception is that the state has a lien when Medicaid starts to pay benefits. In fact, Medicaid doesn't place a lien on the home until after death. It often can take months, or in the case above where there is a surviving spouse or qualifying child, that lien might not be filed for years.

There are also other scenarios where the state may not seek estate recovery. Under what is known as a hardship exception, if property in the estate is the sole source of income for one or more survivors and pursuing recovery would likely result in those individuals needing public assistance themselves, then the state may not go after assets. Also, if a family member was living in the home before the Medicaid beneficiary died, and continues to make it his/her primary residence, then the state will record a lien but wait until the property is either sold or the family member dies or moves out before seeking repayment.

Those are the basics. But, you've probably got a whole bunch of questions about how the whole process works. For example, what exactly is counted as part of the estate? Some states define it narrowly to mean the probate estate, that is, property that passes by way of the estate administration process. But other states have expanded that definition to include any property that belonged to the Medicaid recipient at the time of death, including jointly held property and assets held in trust. Life insurance proceeds would not be included where there is a specifically named beneficiary. On the other hand, they would be included if the estate is the beneficiary.

What if there aren't enough assets in the estate to pay the lien and other expenses? Medicaid gets a priority, getting paid right after reasonable funeral expenses and costs of estate administration, along with taxes and ahead of other creditors and heirs. The law requires the executor or administrator to contact the state to find out if any money is owed.

But, as with many laws and regulations, the estate recovery laws may not work so smoothly in practice. Let's say Dad is on Medicaid and Mom owns the home. Dad dies but Mom is still alive. No estate recovery yet. The state must wait until she dies. But, what if Mom lives another five, ten, or twenty years? The home may no longer be in Mom's name. If she sold it and spent the money on her own care, then no problem. That's what the state wants. However, what if she transfers the home out of her name? Can the state enforce a lien in that case? And, how would they even know when to file a lien? Maybe they would know if a will is probated. But, if that's not the case, then most likely the state won't know of Mom's death. And there doesn't appear to be any requirement to notify Medicaid of Mom's death unless she, too, received Medicaid.

So, what would happen in that case? Many of these questions may take time to answer as these different scenarios play out over a number of years. This is just another example of why it is so difficult to navigate the long-term care system.

Chapter 3

Medicaid—The Application

The Risk of Going the Medicaid Application Process Alone

When money is running out and the family is faced with the need to apply for Medicaid to pay for long-term care, the question becomes, "Should we do this ourselves or should we hire an elder law attorney to help?" Sometimes the hospital or the nursing home tells the family they will qualify without too much difficulty. So they try to do it themselves.

The pitfalls of going it alone are many and varied, especially since the latest round of Medicaid changes, effective February 2006, made the laws and regulations in this area much more complicated. Timing is critical. By that, I mean to say that when you spend down assets, and what assets you have at a certain point in time, will have an impact on qualifying for benefits. Let me illustrate by way of example.

Karl and Linda were in their eighties and living in their home, which they owned. They had other countable assets of approximately $50,000. Karl and Linda had done no planning for their long-term care needs. Karl became ill in October, was admitted to the hospital and then to a nursing home for rehabilitative services. His condition was such, that he could not go home and needed to stay in the nursing home on a long-term basis, at a private-pay cost of $10,000 per month.

Linda was told by various personnel at the hospital and the nursing home that based on their level of assets "Karl would qualify for Medicaid" in January and they arranged for her to meet with a Medicaid caseworker to make an application for benefits. Being stressed out by the reality that Karl would not go home and uncomfortable with the complicated process she did not understand that for Karl to qualify she would have to spend down a portion of their assets to get below a certain dollar amount. In her case that number was $27,000. The caseworker explained this to her at the interview but, quite frankly, she was receiving so much information, she really didn't fully understand how important that was.

Linda waited for medical and nursing home bills to come in. She figured she owed the money so it was as good as spent. In other words, in her mind she didn't have $50,000. They owed $28,000 so she had $22,000 left. Not true under Medicaid rules. Until she wrote those checks, Karl and Linda were "overresourced," Medicaid's term for having too much money to qualify for benefits. If you are overresourced by even a dollar, you won't get Medicaid for that month. You will never get Medicaid for that month.

Had she paid those bills right away, Karl would have qualified for benefits in January. Instead, Linda didn't write those checks until June, meaning Karl didn't qualify for Medicaid until July. Great, so Medicaid picked up the nursing home bill in July. There was one small problem. Who was going to pay the bill for January through June? The answer was Karl and Linda, and at the private-pay rate of $10,000 per month, that was $60,000. The shame is that this didn't need to happen.

This example illustrates the pitfalls of going it alone. The rules are quite complicated, and timing is critical. You don't want to be left with a huge nursing home bill that you can't pay. The nursing home doesn't really want to be in the position of suing their residents. Having a knowledgeable, elder law attorney representing you can save huge dollars and huge amounts of stress.

So, how did Karl and Linda's problem get resolved? She hired us to negotiate with the nursing home. We were able to reduce the bill a little bit, and since she only had $22,000 in liquid assets and could not afford to pay the bill now, the home agreed to take a mortgage against her home. They'll get paid when the home is sold. Not the best end result, but as good as could be expected.

A Medicaid Story that Starts Out Badly but Turns Out Just Fine

Let's take a look at a Medicaid success story, one in which we were able to work to fix the mistakes that were made long before long-term care and Medicaid were needed. Susie contacted me concerning her mom, who was living in an assisted-living facility with an aide, which she and her sisters were paying for with cash. Mom had transferred her assets to her three daughters. They had begun to spend some of the money on Mom's care, but had also opened and closed accounts, moving, combining, and commingling assets. Over time, it was difficult to follow the paper trail and establish with Medicaid that Mom's money had been spent for her care, and not gifted to the children. Susie, however, reached out to me within a few months after the initial transfers and almost two years before we applied for Medicaid.

We quickly counseled Susie that the assets had to be returned, and thankfully, although some had been spent on Mom's care, she and her sisters still had possession of the balance. We then guided Susie on the records that she needed to obtain in preparation for the anticipated Medicaid application. While she still employed the aide, we were able to prepare invoices and documentation showing that the cash withdrawals were not gifts, but payment for services, including a statement from the facility. Susie had been paying the facility bill on her credit card and then taking money from Mom's account (which was titled in Susie's name). We had her go back through her records and copy the credit card bills with those charges and match up payments back to her from "Mom's account." We also counseled her on a better way to make those payments.

Finally, Susie and her sisters had moved money from one account to another, for convenience, a better interest rate, or to keep FDIC insurance coverage. Without recognizing it, however, they were muddying the paper trail. You see, Medicaid requires as many as five years of financial records to show how money has been spent. Susie and her sisters didn't realize the problems they were creating. We painstakingly had to document all the transfers from one account to another, and transfers in and out of each account.

As I said, this was a success story. We applied for Medicaid, walked the caseworker through the details of each and every transaction, backed by supporting documentation, and the family received Medicaid approval without a hitch. Every dollar had been accounted for, and we achieved a smooth transition to Medicaid with no ineligibility period. Financially, the family can rest easy that Mom's care is paid for and the nursing facility, which receives those Medicaid benefits, is happy that their resident went from private pay to Medicaid without interruption of payment. This is an example of the way things can work if you have someone with knowledge guiding you through the process.

Assisted-Living Medicaid—The Risks of "Going It Alone"

The rules governing Medicaid aren't uniform. Different rules may apply to different Medicaid programs. A recent case we handled in our office illustrates this point.

John had been in an assisted-living facility for several years. His wife, Nancy, was living at home and private paying for his care. She had numerous conversations with the assisted-living facility about Medicaid, and was told that qualifying wouldn't be a problem and that John could remain in the facility on Medicaid. Pretty simple—or so it seemed.

Nancy began the long winding journey that we have come to know as the Medicaid application process. Nancy did not understand the timing aspect of Medicaid, that she had to reach a target level of assets before John could qualify, and that each month she missed that target was a lost month, never to be recaptured. This was of paramount importance to her, since she is several years younger than John and will need to preserve as much as she can to live on after he is gone.

The Medicaid application process dragged on as the caseworker asked for each follow-up piece of documentation, which was all very confusing to Nancy. She finally sought assistance, and we were able to help her finally achieve financial eligibility. At that point, Medicaid sent a nurse out to the facility to evaluate John medically in order to determine that he needed nursing home care. Mission accomplished. John received the go-ahead. Now, all that remained was for the facility to complete its required form, indicating that it would OK John for a Medicaid slot. Imagine the surprise when we received word of Medicaid's denial!

We followed up, only to learn that the facility refused to make a Medicaid slot available, despite the promises made to John and Nancy. However, we were told by Medicaid that John could still be approved if the facility simply changed its stance and made a room available.

John and Nancy's experience is a cautionary tale for families. Qualifying for Medicaid is anything but simple, especially when it comes to assisted living. It requires the cooperation of families and the facilities caring for their loved one. It is confusing and time consuming, and best not handled without the guidance of a qualified professional, such as an elder law attorney. And keep in mind that much of this is state specific.

Although the long-term care options are complicated no matter where you live, each state has its own system and set of laws, so make sure you consult with someone familiar with the process in the state where your loved one lives.

Why Pay Someone to File a Medicaid Application I Can Complete Myself?

The call usually starts out this way. "I've given all of Dad's money to the nursing home already and am ready to apply for Medicaid. His situation is really simple. I can handle it myself, but I just have a few questions."

I'm always happy to try to help whenever I can, but when I tell people that doing it yourself can often cause a loss of tens or even hundreds of thousands of dollars, they act surprised. A recent case we handled in our office will illustrate this point.

Jill called us regarding her dad, who was in the hospital, ready to be transferred to a nursing home. She had picked out a nursing home, applied for Medicaid, and thought she had a plan in place. Dad would move to the home, private pay for a few months, and then apply for Medicaid. Then, she got a letter from Medicaid stating that Dad had made a number of asset transfers that made him ineligible for benefits. The caseworker requested copies of checks and documents explaining deposits and withdrawals before he could tell Jill how long Dad's penalty would be. Jill called us in desperation.

Now, I have to tell you that some of the most challenging cases we get are those where we haven't done the planning for families, or even filed the Medicaid application but rather are called in to finish a process that has suddenly been derailed. And that, unfortunately, was what happened to Jill. The nursing home she lined up for Dad learned of the Medicaid problems and said she needed to get them straightened out before they could admit him. We took a look at the details, and here is what we discovered.

Dad had transferred his home to his children ten years earlier. That wasn't the problem. However, Dad was still living there and paying much of the expenses of the home, but doing so by way of reimbursing Jill, who was actually paying the taxes, insurance, etc. Additionally, Dad had been giving money to his children over the past several years. Hardly unusual, but transfers subject to a penalty, nonetheless. Finally, Jill had been using Dad's bank account to deposit some of her own funds. She did this out of convenience, but didn't realize what a problem it would cause when Medicaid counted it as Dad's.

The questionable transfers totaled almost $75,000, a ten-month Medicaid penalty if we couldn't prove otherwise. So, we rolled up our sleeves and got to work. We learned that Jill's brother Bill was disabled. Transfers to a disabled child are exempt from the transfer rules (something Jill didn't know and which never came up at the Medicaid interview). That reduced the questionable transfers to $50,000.

We then painstakingly went through the five years of account statements and had Jill provide us with as much information as possible to piece together the entire picture of money going in and out of Dad's account. We separated what was actually Jill's, and proved it to Medicaid. Most of the payments that Dad made relating to the home he no longer owned we also were able to get Medicaid to treat as reasonable home expenses.

All this helped to reduce the $75,000 down to $20,000, resulting in a three-month penalty. Dad entered the nursing home, the family private paid for three months, and then Medicaid kicked in. The net savings to the family by knocking seven months off the penalty was $70,000. Not knowing the Medicaid ins and outs, Jill would have never been able to do it on her own. Yes, she filled out the application, but it was the rest of the complicated process she needed our help with.

Chapter 4

Medicaid — The Strategies

Crisis Planning — Nothing Left But the House

Increasingly, we are receiving calls with the following common fact pattern. Mom and Dad are still living in their home, which they own. They both need around-the-clock nursing home–level care, and have home health aides living with them. This has been going on for a number of years, and they have spent down all their assets on care and maintaining the home. Now, the children are spending their own money, in some cases as much as $10,000 per month, with no end in sight. They want to sell the home, but in today's economy and real estate market that isn't as easy as it once was. Their current predicament is taxing on the family, both financially and emotionally. Is there any way out?

Actually, there is. There is a way to move both parents into a nursing home, get them on Medicaid, and reimburse the children for monies they paid for their parents' care. Medicaid rules are very complex, and the timing of each step in the process is critical, but it can be done. Here's how it works.

The first step is to get one of the parents into a nursing home. Let's say it's Dad. If he is in the hospital already (often the case when we get the call), then he should be transferred from there to the nursing home. We then apply for Medicaid. The house is an exempt asset (i.e., not a countable asset for Medicaid eligibility purposes) since Mom is still living there. Once we get Dad approved for Medicaid, there is what is called a "division of assets." Whatever is Mom's is now hers, to be spent on her care, but not on Dad's. This is the key.

So, then we work on getting Mom into a nursing home, and then apply for Medicaid for her. The home will have to be sold (unless there is a family member living there), but it won't hold up Mom's Medicaid—which is important, since it's not so easy these days to sell in what is now considered a down market. Once the home is sold, Mom will lose her eligibility for Medicaid and will need to private pay from the proceeds of the sale. She could also keep her Medicaid eligibility and pay the proceeds to the state to reimburse it for benefits paid up until that point. Which option is better depends on how much is realized from the sale and how much is owed to the state. But keep in mind that the state pays the nursing home at a lower rate than you or I would pay (approximately 50% less).

And what about the money that the children paid out of their own pocket for Mom and Dad's care? They can be reimbursed from the proceeds once they sell the house. However, everything must be documented because Medicaid presumes that transfers between family members are gifts, not loans. If it is a loan, then there must be a written agreement. The best practice is for there to be a recorded mortgage. At the closing, the mortgage is paid off and a discharge is recorded by the buyer's attorney. The children are reimbursed directly and there is a record as far as Medicaid is concerned.

In the end, the parents are paying for their care from their own assets, the children are paid back (money that they will need for their own retirement and long-term care needs), and depending on how much long-term care is needed and what the home sells for, there may even be some amount left to transfer to the next generation in the form of an inheritance.

The Home—To Transfer or Not to Transfer

Home ownership has long been a large part of the American dream. Through the course of the twentieth century, the percentage of Americans owning their homes rose considerably. In many of these homes, three generations lived under one roof. Today, there are still many three-generation homes. The reasons for it are often the same, e.g., the grandparents often help care for their grandchildren while the parents are working, sometimes the grandparents need assistance and can't live alone any longer, etc.

There is, however, a big difference between the households of the twentieth century and those of the twenty-first century—which generation owns the home. The parent homeowner of the twentieth century now is the grandparent homeowner of the twenty-first century.

So, now that homeowner, we'll call him Oscar, is in his seventies. His son Paul, Paul's wife, and their kids live with Oscar. They are concerned that as Oscar ages and needs long-term care, they may lose the house. Paul wants to buy a house, but can't afford it, even in today's depressed real estate market. So they come upon a solution. Oscar will transfer his house to Paul, or perhaps sell to Paul at a reduced price, maybe just enough to pay off Oscar's mortgage. Paul will have a home of his own in which to raise his family, and Oscar will have the support of family should he need it. A win-win scenario for everyone, right?

Well, not so fast. If Paul doesn't pay fair market value for the home, then the uncompensated amount is treated as a transfer for less than fair value should Oscar need Medicaid benefits in the next five years to pay for long-term care.

What to do? Oscar and Paul must understand that if Oscar needs care, there must be a plan in place to cover the cost of that care. That plan could involve VA benefits if Oscar is a veteran. It could also include using Oscar's funds to pay for his care, and long-term care insurance benefits. But if these sources of payment still leave a gap, then Paul will need to borrow against the home to pay for Oscar's care, which may mean putting off tapping into the equity to pay for renovations or other expenses.

Provided these contingencies are covered, however, the home transfer can work well. But what happens, however, if Oscar is not healthy when contemplating a transfer, but instead has dementia and already needs some care? In that case, the home transfer is a little more complicated. It is possible that within five years he will need nursing home care, so we are concerned about the five-year Medicaid look back. What options do Oscar and Paul have?

One possibility is for Paul to buy the home at a price that he can afford, but that may be below fair market value. If, for example, he purchases the home for $200,000 and it is worth $450,000, then $250,000 is considered a gift subject to the Medicaid transfer penalty. Oscar can spend down the $200,000 for his care, but if he runs out of money, then Paul may need to cover the cost of care until the five-year time frame expires.

Now that Oscar lives in Paul's home, they could enter into an agreement for Oscar to pay rent. If Paul or his wife is providing care that Oscar otherwise would need to hire an aide to do, then Oscar could pay them to do it. This is what is called a personal services contract. Food, utilities, and other goods and services that Paul may be providing can and should be paid for by Oscar. Perhaps the home needs to be modified to allow Oscar to live there. Paul could spend money to make those improvements when they become necessary, borrowing against the home.

Some or all of these strategies may be ways for Paul to, in essence, pay Oscar for some of the remaining uncompensated value of Oscar's home, over time, in a way that may be more affordable for Paul. However, each of these financial arrangements must be in writing. This is because Medicaid presumes that any transfer of money or services is a gift, subject to a transfer penalty, unless it is in writing and at fair value.

But a word of caution—the Medicaid rules are complicated. What will work in one state may not work in another. What may be suitable for one family may be entirely the wrong solution for another. If you try to do it yourself and get it wrong, you may find yourself with a lengthy period of Medicaid ineligibility and no money to pay for care. Better to seek professional help from an experienced and trusted elder law attorney to help you navigate through the maze of laws and regulations that leave hidden traps for the unwary.

What is a "Step Up in Basis" and Why Do I Want to Keep It?

"Mom wants to transfer her home to me. Do you think it's a good idea?" Although this is a seemingly simple question, it is probably one of the more common questions I am asked as an elder law attorney. But not one that I can answer without knowing more about the people involved. One size does not fit all.

The home is typically the largest asset people have, and they are frequently and understandably emotionally attached to it. The primary residence also enjoys special tax treatment, and that is what most people fail to consider when they make this kind of decision. Let's run through the basics.

Real estate, like stocks, bonds, and other investments, is subject to capital gains tax. If Mom bought her home for $100,000 and sells it for $500,000, she has what is called a "realized gain," and Uncle Sam will want to tax her on that gain. The gain is calculated by taking the amount she sold the home for and subtracting the "cost basis," her purchase price plus capital improvements (e.g., addition, new roof, windows, siding), and closing costs.

In my example, if Mom made no improvements, her gain is $400,000. The capital gains tax she must pay is based on her tax bracket. The higher the bracket she's in, the higher the tax will be, although capital gains tax rates are lower than the rates for regular income. Let's say her tax rate is 20%; therefore, her potential capital gains tax is $80,000. I say "potential" because if the home was her primary residence in two of the five years before she sold it, then she can exclude up to $250,000 of gain. Married couples can exclude $500,000 of gain.

If Mom transfers her home to me and I don't make it my primary residence, then when I sell it I won't be able to exclude any capital gains from tax. But, Mom still intends to live in the home. I don't want to sell it until after she passes away. Is there a way to avoid the capital gains tax entirely?

Yes, by invoking something called the "step up in basis." If Mom owns the home when she dies and passes it to me upon her death, my cost basis when I sell is not what she paid for it, but rather what it was worth at the time of her death (or, alternatively, six months after her death). If I sell it immediately after she dies, my capital gains is zero, and thus there is no tax. On the other hand, if I sell after Mom dies, but she transferred it to me during her lifetime, then I owe Uncle Sam capital gains tax.

So, then that's it, right? Mom shouldn't transfer the home to me. Well, not so fast. What if Mom gets sick and needs long-term care? Capital gains tax, at worst, will never consume the entire proceeds of the sale. Long-term care, however, could easily exceed the home's value if it is needed for several years. But do I have to really choose between the two? Well, maybe there is another way.

Putting the home in a trust, if set up properly, can accomplish both goals. The home is removed from the parent's name, and if done five years or more before needing long-term care, will be outside the Medicaid look back, the time frame within which Medicaid looks to confirm that you have in fact spent all your money and haven't given it away. At the same time, the trust can be set up in such a way that the assets it holds will be part of Mom's estate, and she will be able to take advantage of both the capital gains tax exclusion and the step up in basis.

We accomplish the best of both worlds. The home can be protected, and tax advantages will not be lost. But, there are even more potential benefits. Since the home is not in the child's name but in the trust, it is not subject to the child's creditors, or to being split with the child's spouse in a divorce. Additionally, if Mom needs care within five years of the transfer, the home can be sold or borrowed against to help pay the cost of care. In other words, some of the asset can be used for care but not all of it need be consumed.

As you can see, it was a simple question, or so you thought. Is home transfer right for you and your family? Well, that depends on many factors, including the health of the parent, what other assets exist to pay for long-term care, and what goals the parent and child want to accomplish. One thing is for sure. Planning early makes things easier and the outcome so much better than waiting until a crisis hits.

How Home Ownership Can Be a Benefit in a Medicaid Spend-Down Scenario

Iris's husband, Harry, had been in and out of hospitals and nursing homes, and a permanent nursing home stay was looking more than likely. Their assets totaled approximately $150,000 (not including their home and one car, both of which are "exempt" for Medicaid purposes). Iris went to the Medicaid office to see what benefits would be available to help her pay for her husband's nursing home costs. The caseworker explained to Iris that, upon application for Medicaid benefits, the state will total all of the assets she and Harry own on the day he entered the nursing home (the "snapshot date"), divide by two, and that is what Iris is entitled to keep, but only up to a maximum of $109,560. Harry will qualify for Medicaid once he spends his "half" of the assets down below $2,000.

Iris and Harry, therefore, needed to spend their assets down to $77,000 (150,000 ÷ 2 + 2000) before qualifying Harry for benefits. Iris was distraught at the idea of having to spend her life savings ... what about her own health-care costs? A social worker at the hospital recommended that Iris contact an elder law attorney to see if there are ways they could preserve more of their assets. When we met Iris, we explained that there was a way she would be able to increase the amount of assets she is entitled to keep. Here is how.

Iris and Harry owned their home free and clear, with no mortgage. It was no problem for them to take a home equity line of credit in the amount of $100,000, since their home was worth approximately $400,000. Iris immediately borrowed $70,000 against the line, before Harry entered the nursing home. By doing so, she increased the amount of assets at the snapshot date from $150,000 to $220,000. This meant that Iris could keep $109,560, and the couple would need to spend the remaining assets down to $2,000. In other words, the couple would have to spend $110,440 before Harry could qualify for nursing home benefits.

After Harry entered the nursing home, we instructed Iris to repay the line of credit, leaving another $40,440 to spend down. Paying the nursing home and other bills quickly accomplished that, and we were able to get Harry Medicaid. The end result was that Iris kept nearly $110,000 of their combined $150,000, much-needed money considering she was also going to lose some of Harry's income and could very well outlive him by five years or more.

A word of caution: This scenario is fact specific to Iris and Harry and should not be considered without proper legal counseling. The bottom line is that before you start spending down, you should seek advice from someone who knows the Medicaid laws.

Some Married Couple Spend-Down Options to Consider

Kate and Larry own their home and have $150,000 in savings. They have wills leaving everything to each other and then alternatively to their children, but they have done nothing to address their long-term care needs. Larry is now about to enter a nursing home, and Kate is faced with spending down to $75,000 and losing Larry's income before he will be eligible for Medicaid. This is a classic crisis planning case. Does Kate have any options?

Actually, yes. Although she will have to spend down her assets, there are ways to spend that will be more beneficial for Kate. Let's go through a list of some of them.

At the top of the list is setting up an irrevocable burial fund to pay for both of their funerals. Better to do that now. Otherwise, she'll have to take that expense out of what Medicaid says she can keep. Other strategies focus on exempt assets, e.g., the house and a car. Kate will keep the house and one car. Of the $75,000 that she has to spend down, she could fix up the house. That might include replacing an old cooling or heating system, installing new windows and/or siding, and remodeling the interior. If she makes improvements that enhance the value of the home, should she decide to sell, that will result in more money for her to live on.

How about her car? Kate has a ten-year old car. It is better for her to purchase a new car as part of the spend down. Or perhaps she has a car loan that she is paying off over time. Paying it off before applying for Medicaid may be the better alternative. That also applies for other debt, such as credit cards or other installment loans. Finally, Kate ought to look at anticipated expenses. For example, if she or Larry needs dental work, now may be the time to do it.

Some of the spend down will need to go to the nursing home to pay for the cost of care at its private-pay rate; therefore, it is important to determine what amount will be necessary to get Larry into a quality facility. Knowing that, they can then work backward to determine what they have left to spend on the other items. Additionally, if Larry is not yet in the hospital or nursing home, it may be possible for Kate to keep more than $75,000 by taking a home equity line of credit.

A word of caution, however: One size does not fit all. What is best for one person may not be right for another. Medicaid rules are very complicated and quite technical. Before taking any action, it is best to consult with an elder law attorney well versed in Medicaid law. But, if done properly, Kate can preserve more than the 50% of assets that Medicaid laws say she can keep. This is especially important, given the possibility that Kate may outlive Larry by five or ten years, or more.

How Can the Government Tell Me
I Can't Help My Family?

Sherry had been reading my stories for some time about the need to plan ahead for long-term care. Something struck a chord with her, and she called. She has a home and about $200,000 in investments. Still healthy, she is seventy and thinking about the future. I then asked her if she had made any gifts to her kids or grandkids.

She replied, "No gifts, but I am helping out my son Tim a little bit because he has been out of work for six months."

"Well, Sherry, actually, the money you are giving your son may disqualify you for government benefits down the road, should you need them," I explained.

Sherry became exasperated. "Tim has had such a tough time finding a job in this economy. How can the government tell me I can't help my family when they are in need?"

The reason for this is the Medicaid spend-down rules. The government wants you to spend your money on your own long-term care first, before asking for assistance.

Now, not all your money must be spent on long-term care. But it must be spent in such a way that you are getting something of equal value back.

Sherry heard this and in an exasperated tone cried, "What could provide me greater value and satisfaction than helping to keep a roof over my son's, daughter-in-law's, and grandchildren's heads—and food on the table—until Tim can get back on his feet? My parents helped us out when my husband lost his job. In tough times, our family has always pulled together and pitched in. Tim is a good son. He just needs a break."

While you and I may view Sherry's help as essential and proper, unfortunately, the government does not. Sherry estimates that she has given Tim $50,000 over the last six months and intends to continue to do so. Right now, however, she has a potential Medicaid penalty of about seven months, and that will only increase if she continues to advance funds to Tim.

Sherry is really getting agitated now. "So are you telling me I have to stand by and watch Tim lose his house—that I can't do anything?"

"Not at all," I replied. "You can be there for Tim, but we have to do it in a way that won't create long-term care problems for you down the road." Sherry was all ears.

I told Sherry that we can set up a trust to which she transfers assets. The trust then provides the funds to Tim. Now, you may be thinking, "Doesn't this create the same problem Sherry already has by giving Tim money each month or two?" It does create a potential penalty, but by having Sherry transfer the money in one lump sum, Medicaid's five-year look back is applied one time, so we know when it will expire. If she transfers a little bit at a time, Sherry creates a new five-year look back for each separate transfer.

But isn't there a potential Medicaid penalty when the trust gives money to Tim? No, because Medicaid only looks at Sherry's transfers, not the trust's.

Some may read this and conclude that this is just a way for Sherry to avoid using her money for long-term care and have the government pay her bills instead. But is that really what is going on here? Clearly not. Sherry isn't even thinking about long-term care (although she certainly needs to). Through the use of a trust, she can accomplish both goals, helping her son get back on his feet and providing for her own needs. If she becomes sick, she'll definitely need to use some of her funds for her own care. But when she spends down completely, if done properly, she will be ready for Medicaid. And that benefits not only Sherry, but also the providers of her care who will receive those Medicaid payments, whether it happens to be a nursing home, assisted-living facility, or home health-care agency.

The long-term care provider will know that after Sherry spends down her assets, she will qualify for Medicaid without any surprise ineligibility periods imposed by Medicaid. And Sherry will know that she can be there for her family and still meet her own needs. Mission accomplished.

How We Saved a Family $240,000

Rhoda called because she was flat out of money and desperate. Dad had been in a nursing facility for almost four years now. He had spent down his money, and Rhoda had paid the $11,000-per-month expense after that, until she was tapped out of her home equity line of credit to the tune of $240,000. Dad owned a home, which Rhoda had always figured she would eventually sell and reimburse to herself the money she had advanced. She was panicked, however, after someone told her that she might not get that money back because Medicaid would "take the house." She called us after a friend told her to speak with an elder law attorney.

Rhoda definitely had a problem. Although Medicaid doesn't "take" the home, when Dad starts to receive Medicaid benefits, the state runs a tab, so to speak. That tab comes due when he dies, under what is called estate recovery, and the state will get paid first when the home is sold because Rhoda didn't have a mortgage to protect her $240,000 loan to Dad. So, each month that Dad receives Medicaid benefits is money that Rhoda will lose, because the house is only worth $250,000. I told Rhoda not to worry. I had a solution, but we had to work quickly before we filed a Medicaid application. Here's what we did.

Rhoda had no problem documenting the payments on Dad's behalf. The nursing facility provided us with a payment history as well. We first had Rhoda and Dad enter into a loan agreement backed by a mortgage, which we recorded, on Dad's home. A realtor provided us with document-tation showing that Rhoda had listed Dad's home for sale for about a year and had to continually lower the asking price, which was now $250,000. We needed this to establish the fair market value.

Rhoda then entered into a contract to purchase Dad's home for $250,000. We represented Dad, and Rhoda hired her own attorney. It had to be what attorneys refer to as an "arm's length transaction," with all the usual realty transfer fees and recording costs. Rhoda's payment for the home was the $240,000 she paid to the nursing home plus Dad's closing costs (which she paid).

Finally, we applied for Medicaid, disclosing all the above transactions. Medicaid definitely examined it closely. But we had the documentation to back everything up. This was not a case of Dad gifting Rhoda $250,000. Rhoda had paid full value for the home, and Dad had used the money to pay for his care. In the end, I am proud to say, Medicaid approved our application and Rhoda did get back her $240,000. And the state can't be unhappy either, since Dad used every last dollar for his care before reaching out for government benefits.

Rhoda was lucky, but I don't recommend waiting as long as she did to reach out for help. Had she handled the Medicaid application herself, she likely would have lost tens of thousands of dollars, and possibly all of the money she spent. And since Rhoda is sixty-five, that's money she'll need for her own care needs in the not-too-distant future.

How a Call from Ann's Attorney
Saved Her $90,000

One of the common themes I repeat often, when it comes to Medicaid, is that timing is everything. A recent call we received from Ann's personal injury attorney, Bill, illustrates this point. Ann's husband, Ted, has dementia and is about to enter a nursing home. Ann and Ted don't have much in the way of assets, about $100,000, but Bill is pursuing a claim on Ann's behalf for injuries she received in a car accident. Bill, recognizing the potential Medicaid issues, called me to ask if Ted's situation impacts Ann's claim. I told him he reached out to me at the right time. Here's why.

In the case of a married couple, Medicaid considers the assets of both the healthy and ill spouse in determining eligibility. The question then becomes, "At what point in time do we value their assets?" That is what is called the snapshot date. Medicaid values the assets as of the first day of the first month of continuous institutionalization. Bill told me that he was close to settling Ann's case, and asked whether pushing the case to settle would be helpful.

I explained that if Ann receives the settlement proceeds before Ted is approved for Medicaid it would count as part of the spend down, and she would only be able to keep, at most, half the money. We don't want the case to settle until after Ted gets Medicaid because at that point there is a "division of assets." Ann keeps the $50,000 of assets that they have left after the spend down, along with whatever other assets she receives after that date.

Once Bill understood the best sequence of events, he recommended that Ann contact us to guide her on how to spend down and to handle the Medicaid application. And that's what we did. In a few months time, Ted received Medicaid, Ann kept $50,000 of their savings, and then Bill settled the case, providing Ann with $90,000 of additional funds to support her— money she especially needs since most of Ted's income must be paid to the nursing home. So, when we talk about timing being everything, in Ann's case it meant an extra $90,000 in her pocket.

Can I Be Paid to Provide Care for Mom?

In times of crisis, families pull together. Long-term care is no different. So much of the care is administered by family members. And it doesn't take too long before the question is asked, "Can I be paid to care for my mom or dad?" A recent New Jersey court case makes it clear how tricky that can be.

Mom was ninety-seven years old and in a nursing home. The daughter, let's call her Jean, entered into a caregiver contract with Mom to provide care, and was paid the sum of $56,000. This amount was based on Jean performing fifteen hours per week at a rate of $25 per hour for 2.9 years, the life expectancy of a ninety-seven-year-old. The payment was made, and within five years of that payment Mom applied for Medicaid. The state denied her application, counting the $56,000 as a transfer for less than fair value, not a payment for fair value received.

We use life care contracts often in the cases in our office. These are agreements in which one family member agrees to provide care to another family member for a fee. But we also know that the state will scrutinize those contracts very closely because when the payments are going to family members, the state assumes that these transfers are "for less than fair value," what most people would call gifts. They will then impose a penalty period—a period of ineligibility.

For example, the contract can't be retroactive. If I have been caring for Mom for the last two years and now we decide that it would be a good idea for her to pay me for that care, Medicaid will flag that transfer. I had no expectation that I would be paid when I performed the services so I can't change that now. There must be a contract in place going forward. I also can't be paid an outrageous sum of money. Mom can pay me no more than what are fair market rates for the services I will perform.

So why didn't our ninety-seven-year-old Mom get Medicaid? A big problem with this contract was the fact that it was a lump sum payment. Jean was paid $56,000 before she even performed a single hour of service. Now, this was necessary in order to spend down to below $2,000 for Mom to be under the Medicaid asset limit. And every attempt was made to calculate an amount that was based on fair market rates. In fact, the rate was at the low end of that scale.

However, there were other parts of the contract that the court found objectionable. For example, the contract stated that the caregiver was not obligated to devote full time to care since Jean had a career and family to attend to. She would devote as much time as she could to providing care. The contract anticipated the average amount of time would be fifteen hours or more per week. The contract also stated that the $56,000 due under the contract was not dependent on the exact amount of time Jean worked, and that if Mom canceled the contract, Jean would be paid under the assumption she had worked fifteen hours per week.

The court found the contract to be one-sided. Jean was not obligated to perform any minimum amount of services. Her compensation was not tied to actual performance. In a normal commercial transaction, would anyone pay for something without being sure what they were going to receive? And although the court didn't specifically mention it, I think the fact that Mom was in a nursing home and not at home receiving care may have also had something to do with its decision. The nursing home was providing 24/7 care, so what Jean would provide in the way of services was even less certain.

So, does this mean that a child can't be paid for providing care to a parent? Absolutely not. But the line between what works and what doesn't isn't a black-and-white one. That's why cases like this help us define it with a bit more clarity so that we, as elder law attorneys, can help our clients decide what the best course of action is in their particular situation as we guide them through what we call the elder care journey.

Is My Family Business at Risk Because of Long-Term Care?

Steve built his construction business from nothing. He was able to provide for his family, put his children through college, and live a nice life on the income generated from it. Now in his seventies, Steve doesn't work much anymore. He visits his office a few days a week, and receives a paycheck, but has turned over the day-to-day operations to his sons, who have expanded the business. But recent heart surgery and his good friend's recent diagnosis of Alzheimer's disease has caused Steve to consider what will happen if he needs long-term care. Is his business in jeopardy?

The answer to that is yes. You see, Steve still owns 100% of the business. He estimates that it is probably worth close to $750,000. He also owns the building in which his company is housed, and that is probably valued at another $500,000. He receives rental income from his business and from three other tenants there. He and his wife, Alice, have other investments totaling $200,000. Steve figures that if he or Alice needs long-term care, he'll use the investments. When that's gone, he'll still have the salary plus rental income, and his sons will pay for the rest of their care at home through the business.

But is this realistic? What Steve doesn't realize is that 24/7 long-term care averages about $125,000 per year. If both Steve and Alice need care, that's a quarter of a million dollars a year. When I explain this to Steve, he quickly tells me that there is no way the business can support that kind of expense. Quite frankly, what business can? Steve also tells me that he and Alice don't have long-term care insurance. If they can still get it, I would strongly urge them to purchase it. But if they can't get it—what then?

Steve tells me that he doesn't want to sell the business or the building. He has a will that leaves both to his sons.

But, I explain, if he needs long-term care, he will have to sell both before he or Alice can qualify for Medicaid. Steve becomes exasperated.

"My sons support their families through the business, just as I did. I can't sell it now."

I hear what he is saying. More than simply an asset, the business is also the income that supports three families. Yet, Medicaid doesn't look at it that way, which is why Steve ought to strongly consider transferring both the business and the building out of his name now. Careful consideration must be paid to the tax consequences, but by using some of the strategies we have discussed previously, this can protect Steve and his family.

Medicaid transfers carry a five-year look back, so the time to start transferring is now, while Steve and Alice are still healthy. There are gift and estate tax consequences to making transfers. For 2011 and 2012, Steve and Alice can make lifetime gifts of up to $5,000,000 each before having to pay gift tax, so they should be able to transfer these assets without paying tax. They may also be able to eliminate the possibility of estate taxes by employing certain tax strategies.

If Steve wants to continue to receive the income generated by each asset, he has some options. He could transfer ownership to a trust that is set up so that he receives the income from anything held in the trust. On the other hand, he can choose to continue to receive a salary from the business and rental income from the building as an employee. He'll need to consult with his tax advisor to see which way is best.

But by putting a plan in place now to protect both he and Alice, should they need long-term care, he is also preserving the financial viability of his company, which is critical to three generations of his family. This is just another example of how long-term care has the potential to destroy a family unless you take the steps to prepare for it, with the goal of protecting your assets.

Dad Gets German Reparations Money—
Does Mom Get to Keep It?

Jerry's dad receives a monthly check from the German government, compensation as a result of his suffering at the hands of the Nazis in World War II. Dad has dementia and will soon need nursing home care. Jerry is trying to preserve as much as he can for Mom, who is ten years younger than Dad and still in pretty good health.

His question to me was, "Is the German reparations money countable for Medicaid purposes"?

This is an interesting question, and one that could have a real impact on Mom's financial well-being. That's because, under community spouse resource allowance rules, Mom will be able to keep a maximum of $110,000, but has to spend down the balance of their $200,000 in assets before Medicaid will cover Dad's care. That's not much to live on, especially if Mom lives another ten years or more.

Medicaid does exempt the German reparations money from income rules, meaning it isn't counted as income for purposes of determining eligibility. But Dad has received over $200,000 from Germany over the course of his lifetime. Can that money be treated as an exempt or noncountable asset under Medicaid rules? If so, then Mom can keep the extra $200,000, which would go a long way toward easing her money worries.

The problem for most recipients is that it isn't easy to identify which assets are from the German pension because the reparations money wasn't segregated. After all, the average person isn't thinking about needing Medicaid years into the future, nor does he/she know the intricacies and specifics of the Medicaid regulations. And there isn't a specific regulation in the state where Dad lives that talks about German reparations anyway, just a federal regulation. (The Medicaid program is governed by a hybrid of federal and state laws and regulations.)

The good news in the case of Jerry's parents, however, is that if the money can be segregated and traced, then there is a very good chance that the entire amount of reparations money can be exempted. To do this, Jerry must document how much Dad received over his life, place that dollar amount in a separate account, and when we apply for Medicaid we must explain that this is the "German reparations" account. This might require some negotiation with the state, but it is well worth the effort. Mom was relieved when we told her this, and we have begun to take steps to make it all happen.

Can I Add My Children's Names to My Bank Account to Protect It from Medicaid?

Eileen comes in to see me. Her husband, Frank, was diagnosed with Alzheimer's five years ago, and the disease has progressed to the point where he needs long-term nursing home care. At the time of the diagnosis, she talked to some family friends and they told her that the way to preserve assets for her own needs and insure that not all the assets would be spent for Frank's care was to add her children's names to her bank accounts and mutual funds. The accounts would be protected from the Medicaid spend-down provisions. Now that Frank is in a nursing home, she wonders whether she did the right thing. Unfortunately, she did not.

Medicaid says that adding someone else's name to a bank account or mutual fund does not transfer the ownership on that account. In other words, if Eileen had a bank account with $50,000, and she added her daughter's name to the account, the state would say that she did so for convenience purposes. The entire account still belongs to Eileen. Therefore, even though the child's name has been added, the practical effect, from a Medicaid standpoint, is that there has been no transfer and the entire account still belongs to Eileen.

This is true whether we are talking about bank accounts, certificates of deposit, savings bonds, mutual funds, or any other liquid asset. The law says there is no transfer unless, and until, the child actually takes the money out of the account. Using this same example, if Eileen added her daughter's name to the account five years ago, there has been no gift made. If her daughter later takes some money out of the account and moves it into her own name, then the transfer is made at the time the daughter takes the money out of the account. That's because Eileen no longer has access to the money.

However, this general rule does not apply to real estate. For instance, let's say that Maureen is a widow and she owns a house valued at $200,000. If she adds her son's name to the deed, she has made a completed gift or transfer. Why? Because she has no control over the half she transferred to her son. If she wants to sell the home, for example, she can't do it without her son's agreement. A transfer in the amount of $100,000 would cause Maureen to be ineligible for Medicaid for sixteen months. (The length of the penalty depends on the divisor used in your state.) Once that penalty has expired, however, half of the house's value would be protected.

Whether or not it makes sense to add someone's name to real estate or financial accounts depends on the facts and circumstances of each particular case. Adding a name as co-owner also may alter your estate plan, because some of those joint accounts may now pass directly to the surviving owner rather than in accordance with your will.

Long-Term Care Insurance—
How Does Medicaid View It?

Elsie cared for her husband, Max, at home. Max had long-term care insurance to help pay for a home health aide. However, over time, keeping Max at home simply became impossible, and Elsie was forced to place him in a nursing facility. She applied the insurance toward the cost of care there and spent down their assets to cover the balance until she had $100,000 remaining. Elsie then applied for Medicaid—and that's when she ran into a problem, caused, ironically, by the insurance.

Elsie was told that Max's long-term care insurance counts as income, and he therefore had too much income to qualify for Medicaid. Yet, he didn't have enough to cover the private-pay cost of the nursing home. Elsie and Max were caught between a rock and a hard place. How was this possible?

In Max and Elsie's home state of New Jersey, there are two Medicaid programs that cover nursing home care. One program is for applicants who have no more than $2,022 per month in gross income. And when we talk about income, we usually mean Social Security and pension, which can't be modified as long as you live. A second program exists for those who have income greater than $2,022, but the income limit for that program is the equivalent of the Medicaid reimbursement rate. That rate is what Medicaid pays the nursing home, usually somewhere between $5,000 and $6,000, depending on the facility.

Max's insurance policy benefits were being paid directly to him, not to the nursing home. For that reason, Medicaid treated the payments as income to him, which pushed his "income" to $6,500 per month, making him ineligible.

So was that it? Was Elsie out of luck? Not necessarily.

With a slight change, Max could be made eligible. By having the insurance company send the benefit check directly to the nursing home, it would not be counted as income, and he could qualify for Medicaid. That's because, under Medicaid regulations, third-party payments for medical care or services, including room and board, are not counted as income. If the insurance company, as the third party, pays the nursing home directly, then that "income" disappears.

Crazy, right? How can a minor change like that affect Elsie's health and well-being so drastically? It is because Medicaid regulations are so complex and arbitrary. Failing to get the proper guidance can cost literally thousands and hundreds of thousands of dollars. In Elsie's case, she spent another $25,000 before she sought out the advice of an elder law attorney, who helped her fix her application. This is another example of how difficult navigating through the long-term care maze can be and what it might cost you if you don't get it right.

The Right Way and the Wrong Way
to Reduce a Medicaid Penalty

There are many reasons why the Medicaid program is so confusing to the general public. Perhaps the greatest source of misunderstanding is the Medicaid penalty. And that mystification can cost literally thousands to hundreds of thousands of dollars. Allow me to explain.

The Medicaid penalty is actually a period of months of ineligibility for benefits. The more money gifted, or more accurately, "transferred for less than fair value," the longer the penalty. Sounds fairly straightforward—but it isn't. That's because the penalty doesn't actually begin until the applicant files a Medicaid application and the state calculates the penalty.

Many people are entirely in the dark about these rather arcane rules, and they file a Medicaid application only to find out that they will have to transfer money back and spend it down first. And that decision to apply for Medicaid before transfers back are made can be a huge mistake. What if all the money can't be returned? Returning part of the gift should at least reduce the penalty, right?

Well, not necessarily so. Some states don't recognize partial gift returns. Only when all the money is returned will those states wipe out the penalty. And that's one reason I am so fond of telling clients and prospects that timing is everything when it comes to Medicaid.

If Steve can't give back all the money Mom gifted to him, but only part of it, Steve may be better off returning it (for Mom's sake) before she files for Medicaid. Why? Because, remember, the penalty isn't calculated until she applies, and the state reviews her financial records and determines the exact penalty length. A partial return before Mom applies for Medicaid won't result in a reduced penalty because there is only a potential penalty at that point. If Mom transferred $100,000 to Steve, but he transferred half of it back to her, then when she applies for Medicaid the penalty will be calculated on $50,000, not $100,000.

The reduced penalty can save some families tens and hundreds of thousands of dollars and keep them from possible financial ruin. This is another reason why it so important to get proper advice before—preferably years before—an anticipated Medicaid application is to be filed.

Chapter 5

Long-Term Care Planning

Home for the Holidays

In today's society, with families spread across the country, very often family get-togethers are limited to holidays and other life events. It is then that we often visit family members we haven't seen in a while. Changes in older loved ones become more noticeable. It is natural a time for families to face and discuss the difficult decisions about finding care for an older relative. Some of the changes that may indicate your loved one needs some extra help include the following:

1. Weight loss

2. Deterioration in personal hygiene

3. Unusually dirty or messy home

4. Unusually loud or quiet, paranoid, or agitated behavior

5. Local friends and relatives noticing changes in behavior

6. Self-imposed isolation, stops attending activities

7. Signs of forgetfulness, such as unopened mail, piling-up newspapers, missed appointments, unfilled prescriptions

8. Signs of poorly managed finances, such as not paying bills, losing money, paying bills twice

9. Unusual purchases

If you notice changes that are of concern, a physical and neurological exam should identify any medical issues. A geriatric care manager can help assess the options available that will allow your loved one to continue to live a full, fruitful, and safe life. Suggestions may include a home health aide, adult day care, and/or a personal organizer to help with money management.

If your loved one can no longer live alone, possible alternative living arrangements include another family member's home, assisted living, senior housing, or a nursing home. Each choice has pros and cons, and expense is often an issue. Planning should be done as early as possible to determine what government benefits can be tapped to help pay the cost, such as Medicare, Medicaid, and veteran's benefits. A good elder care attorney can provide invaluable assistance and help ensure that you don't run out of money.

All decision-making documents should be examined and updated if necessary. A health-care directive allows another person to make medical decisions for you if you become incompetent. A financial power of attorney allows someone to access your accounts, pay your bills, and conduct other financial transactions for you. Having these documents in place avoids the necessity of going through an expensive, time-consuming, complicated, and emotionally draining court proceeding called a guardianship.

Remember, there are resources available to you. All you need to do is find them or consult with someone knowledgeable, such as an elder care attorney, who can help point you in the right direction.

The Long-Term Care Perfect Storm

Two recent articles in the local paper reminded me again of how a number of forces are combining in the coming years to really make the long-term care issue an acute problem for many Americans, creating a "perfect storm," to use a popular phrase.

As in many states, here in New Jersey, the budget deficit worsens. Our governor announced his state budget for the upcoming year, and many are bracing for cuts in Medicaid programs, a trend that is occurring across the country. The economic recession has reduced tax revenues in many states and caused a reduction in federal funding as well. The federal and state governments contribute, on approximately a fifty-fifty basis, toward the cost of Medicaid programs. What this means is that many states are cutting optional Medicaid programs and reducing the rate at which they reimburse providers.

The second article talks about the first wave of baby boomers who are starting to turn sixty-five in 2011, and the fact that many are postponing their retirement plans for at least four years because of the recession. In other words, they can't afford to retire yet. The article also notes that even before the latest economic downturn, baby boomers were unprepared for retirement, which now typically lasts decades. So, what do you think will happen as 77 million people retire over the next twenty years? Many will enter an overburdened and underfunded long-term care system. More people and less money—a perfect storm indeed.

Knowing this storm is brewing, what can and should you do? I am reminded of *Aesop's Fables*, those stories we all learned as children, specifically the one titled *The Ant and the Grasshopper*. The ant was busy in the summer gathering food and preparing for the coming winter. Meanwhile, the grasshopper was having a good time, with not a care in the world. When winter arrived, he was unprepared and died of starvation.

The same holds true for long-term care planning. Failing to plan while you are healthy may leave you, like the grasshopper, unprepared when a crisis hits. Ask yourself if you could afford an $80,000 to $125,000-per-year additional expense (the average cost of nursing home care), or double those numbers for a married couple, without depleting your assets. If the answer is no, then it may be time to talk to your advisors, including a qualified elder law attorney, about putting a plan in place. Better to be the ant rather than the grasshopper.

The Team Approach to Long-Term Care Planning

Navigating through the long-term care system usually requires a team of advisors. Although the elder law attorney is, no doubt, a pivotal person, the accountant, financial advisor, and insurance specialist are equally important. And when one piece isn't properly in place, it can be catastrophic. Betty's story is illustrative.

Betty and Tom decided to sell their home in which they raised their four children. They invested the majority of the proceeds in annuities and decided to rent and live on the income from their investments and Social Security. Tom, however, had already exhibited some signs of dementia.

After the sale of their home, Tom's condition deteriorated rapidly. He became restless and, at times, physical with Betty, who weighed a hundred pounds less than Tom. She could no longer keep him at home. Betty came to us for help, thinking she could get Tom on Medicaid in a nursing home. She didn't realize that the $300,000 she invested in annuities was now a countable asset and would have to be spent down to $109,560 before Tom could get Medicaid.

Betty was distraught. "I am only sixty-five. How can I live on $100,000?" she asked me.

I told her not to worry. She could cash in the annuities, buy another home with that money, and keep it, as an exempt asset. After Tom qualifies for Medicaid, she could then resell the home if she wanted, to reinvest for income again.

Then we examined the annuities. That's when I discovered the surrender charges of 7% that Betty would have to pay. Although there was a provision that waived the charges if the owner needed to cash them in for long-term care expenses, the problem was that Betty, and not Tom, was the owner. Betty told me that Tom had definitely been diagnosed with dementia at the time that these decisions were made, but couldn't recall any conversations about long-term care or how to provide for it. Big mistake!

We were able to help Betty get Tom into a quality nursing home. She privately paid for seven months, cashed in the annuities, paid a surrender charge, and bought a home. We helped Betty preserve the majority of their savings—money she will need to provide for her own care down the road. But, there are lessons to be learned here.

The result could have been so much better had Betty come to us *before* she sold her home and *before* she bought the annuities. We might have suggested that she wait until Tom entered the nursing home before selling her home. We also would have cautioned Betty about purchasing investments that could easily be liquidated if a large expense (i.e., nursing home care) became necessary. No one thought to ask what would happen if Tom needed care sooner rather than later. And that's why having a team of advisors working together is so important. All tax, financial, and legal aspects of any decision should be analyzed carefully, and that's more than any one advisor is capable of doing.

What Families Need to Know
Before a Crisis Hits

Oftentimes when a new matter comes to our office, the first appointment is not with the parent, but with the children. Commonly, they come to us after or during a crisis, such as a parent's hospital or nursing home stay. Just as often, they have little or no information about what is going on with the parent, either medically or financially, and cannot provide much of the information we need to assist them.

Communication between parent and child before a crisis is so very important and can provide peace of mind and reduce stress for both. The following are some of the questions that families should discuss, which will often begin a dialogue about the type of preplanning parents can do before a crisis occurs.

1. Children should know roughly what and where their parents' assets are. Do they have enough to sustain the healthy spouse should one spouse become ill and need extended hospitalization and/or nursing home care?

2. What does the income picture look like? If one spouse dies, how much income will the surviving spouse be left with? Will there be a significant drop in income? Oftentimes steps can be taken before that spouse dies to help boost the surviving spouse's income.

3. Is financial support anticipated? People are living longer than ever. Many people are at risk of outliving their money. Answering this question means not simply looking at current expenses versus income, but looking at the next step in the elder care journey and the next step after that and asking, "Do I have enough to pay for long-term care? And if so, for how long? And if not, what is my plan then?"

4. What types of insurance are there (i.e., health, long-term care, life)? Is coverage adequate? If not, can coverage be increased? You certainly want to do that before you become uninsurable.

5. Is there a power of attorney and a health-care directive? And where are they? Are they up to date or stale? If these documents are not in place, then the only alternative is a costly and time-consuming process called

guardianship. A court will be involved in your family's affairs, and you may not get the result you want.

6. Is there an up-to-date will? A clear, thought-out estate plan can avoid family squabbles after the parent passes away. Even people with small estates should have a will. Also, make sure the original will can be located. Probating a copy is difficult and expensive.

Is Remaining at Home
Always the Best Option?

In my conversations with families, overwhelmingly, their desire is for elderly family members to remain in their own home as they age and face declining physical and mental health. But is that always the best thing? Perhaps not for everyone.

I was reading a news article that highlighted two cases in which elderly parents were living at home in declining health. One was a ninety-five-year-old woman living in her own home with a team of aides and other assistance, all coordinated by her overwhelmed daughter. The other was an elderly man suffering from Alzheimer's disease, living in the basement of his son's home. The woman had visitors and activity in her home every day. The man did not, spending most of the day alone watching television.

The two cases raise some interesting questions. Would the elderly man be better served in an assisted-living facility or, at least adult day care? He is not getting any mental stimulation through most of the day, which, if received, could slow down the progression of his disease. There is the safety issue as well. He remains at home in the basement for long hours unsupervised. What if there is an emergency? Will help arrive in time?

The elderly woman would seem to be better cared for. She has visitors in and out of her home throughout the day. But her daughter is co-ordinating all this care. It sure sounds like a full-time job. And then we learn that the daughter, herself, is seventy-four years old. How is this affecting her health? And what happens if she needs care? Finally, I wonder what Mom's finances are? All this assistance can approach and exceed the cost of care in a facility. Will she run out of money? And if so, what happens then?

As 77 million baby boomers begin turning sixty-five, long-term care will continue to be a major issue that families will have to wrestle with. And I am not saying that remaining at home shouldn't be the goal for many. However, as with most complex problems, a one-size solution does not fit all. Assisted-living facilities and nursing homes will always have a place in the continuum of care and may be just the right fit for some. Just food for thought—and a different perspective to consider.

Long-Term Care Planning—
A Real-Life Picture

When I speak with people about long-term care and the Medicaid program, I sometimes hear very strong opinions that it is wrong to transfer assets in order to qualify for Medicaid to pay for nursing home care. The person making the statement, however, typically hasn't really given any thought to what that means in real-life situations.

Let me give you an example. Mom is eighty-five years old and living alone. While she clearly shows the signs of aging and should have a plan in place in case she needs long-term care, like most people, she hasn't considered it at all. She received a $100,000 inheritance from her brother. She has always considered her family first, ahead of her own needs, and wants to transfer this inheritance to her son, who is struggling to make ends meet, and just lost his job. She believes she has everything she needs financially, and her maternal instincts are to help her child. You might believe she is being extremely foolish in her thinking, but that is her genuine belief.

Times are tough. Families do what they always do. They pitch in and help each other out. Except that if Mom gives this money to her son and needs nursing home care in the next five years, she won't qualify for Medicaid because of the transfer. So, is Mom trying to beat the system, transferring assets to qualify for Medicaid? No, I think we all would agree that this is not what is motivating her. But it's not that simple. It never is in the real world. Mom ought to be thinking about her own long-term care needs, but she isn't.

Had she consulted with an elder law attorney, she could have set up a plan that would allow her son to receive the inheritance (or she and her son could share the inheritance) by setting up a trust. And when I sat down with Mom and explained to her what would happen if she needs long-term care, she very quickly agreed that it was not a good idea to simply transfer the inheritance to her son. She just had never had that conversation before, and no one ever explained it to her in that way.

So, instead of having that conversation after she received the money, if we had it before the inheritance had been received, my advice to Mom would have been to keep the money in a trust, in case she needs it for long-term care, but that it would be possible to transfer some of it to her son, should he need it. We would have to manage the trust very carefully, but it is clearly doable. I wouldn't call this beating the system. It is a case of families pulling together in times of need. Isn't that what families are supposed to do?

Multigenerational Homes—
A Long-Term Care Solution? Maybe

An article in the newspaper recently caught my attention. It discussed the rising trend of multigenerational households, highlighted by quotes from a few families in which adult children modified their homes so their parents could move in. Looking at it from my perspective as an elder law attorney and knowing from my own experience how unprepared most people are when it comes to long-term care, the article left me with many questions.

According to statistics cited in the article, in 2008 one in six households were multigenerational, up from one in eight thirty years ago. For one family interviewed, the reasons were health related and financial. Dad had a stroke and was forced to retire. Social Security and disability payments aren't enough to pay the costs of maintaining their home, so Daughter and Son-In-Law built an addition. Although not entirely clear, it appears that the children are paying for the addition and the parents will sell their home and live rent free with the children, providing childcare for the grandchildren. The article's author comments that with rising nursing home costs, baby boomer children are increasingly providing care for their parents in their own homes.

But is that realistic in this case? With two toddlers, will Daughter be able to care for her dad if he needs nursing home–level care? Probably not. And is their concern about spending all their money toward a $100,000 a year nursing home bill solved by selling their home? Not at all. Actually, they may have to spend down more by selling their home and living rent free with the kids than if they still owned the home. So, does that mean the decision they made is the wrong one?

Absolutely not. But what it tells me is that they have started to think about and address a very real problem, but haven't gone far enough and thought it all the way through. I certainly don't have all the facts here. But it might make sense for the parents to buy into the home, either now or later. That depends on how much savings they have, who will need long-term care, and when and where it will be administered. The possibility of needing government benefits down the road certainly must be discussed, because what choices the family makes now could very well impact what is available to them later.

Maybe this was all discussed—but experience tells me it probably wasn't. Mom talks in the article about having fewer expenses, and being able to go on vacations and enjoy life. And that is important. But what I see so often is that people don't really look closely at what long-term care means day to day. It means a downward decline in health and an upward trend in expenses. So, you can't just look at where you are now and come up with a solution that solves today's problem. You have to expect your life, in the next ten to twenty years, to look very different from how it is now, and you must plan for that. That's what real long-term care planning is all about.

I've Got a Living Trust, So I've Got Long-Term Care Planning Covered

In discussing long-term care planning with new clients, very often they will tell me that they have everything covered because years earlier they set up a living trust. Living trusts are estate planning devices designed to eliminate the need to probate an individual's estate at his/her death. In the 1990s, they were especially popular and still are very common, especially in states such as Florida and New York, where probate is time consuming and expensive. But are they useful for long-term care planning purposes? Most likely not.

Living trusts are usually revocable, meaning that when a grantor or settlor (the person establishing the trust) transfers assets to it, he or she has the ability to take the assets back out at any point in time. People believe that when they make transfers to the trust, these assets are not counted as theirs for purposes of qualifying for Medicaid or VA Aid and Attendance benefits. That is just plain wrong. If the trust gives you the ability to take the asset back out of the trust, the government will say, "Go ahead and take it back, spend it all down, and then when it is gone come back to us." A trust must be irrevocable, meaning assets transferred to the trust cannot be redistributed directly back to the grantor, for it not to be counted when qualifying for Medicaid.

A second reason living trusts (or other trusts, such as testamentary credit shelter or bypass trusts) won't work for long-term care planning purposes is that they usually contain a clause providing that the trustee can use the assets for the "health support and maintenance" of the beneficiary. Again, if the beneficiary needs long-term care, the government will look at the trust and point to that language. "Long-term care needs are health, support, and maintenance," they'll say, "so spend it down and then come back to us when it's gone."

So, what's the solution? First of all, the trust must be irrevocable. Now, that makes people uncomfortable.

"Does that mean I am giving away my assets and losing control over them?"

The answer of course, is no. What I tell people is that the purpose of this transfer is not to give away assets because you may very well need some (or all) of them, depending on what your health needs are. But you can qualify for government benefits that can help pay for care. Not knowing how long you will live, the challenge is to protect your assets so you don't run out of money. Tapping into other sources helps accomplish that goal because you are spending down your own assets less rapidly.

Additionally, the trust language allowing distribution of assets by the trustee to the beneficiary has to be tailored very carefully so it won't jeopardize eligibility for government benefits. It all adds up to a trust that avoids probate and addresses long-term care planning needs.

The bottom line when it comes to living trusts is to get proper advice before jumping into one, or even if you already have one. Seek the advice of a qualified elder law attorney, who can discuss every option with you. A living trust may meet your particular needs. But then again, it may not.

> **Elder Care Point:** *A trust must be irrevocable, meaning assets transferred to the trust cannot be redistributed directly back to the grantor, for it not to be counted when qualifying for Medicaid.*

The Second Marriage and
How It Impacts Long-Term Care

A very common scenario we see is the case of the late-in-life second marriage. We all need companionship, especially after a spouse has died or after going through divorce. It's lonely being alone. So, we have Andrew and Sally. They marry in their sixties. He has two children from a previous marriage and she has three from her first marriage.

Two years later, Andrew's health starts to deteriorate. It's looking like he will need long-term care. Sally comes to see me.

"I love Andrew, but I am concerned for myself as well," she says. "Will his long-term care needs eat up our assets? We entered into a prenuptial agreement before we married. I had much more financially than he did. So, please review it, and tell me if my assets are protected."

I first explain to Sally that before the prenuptial agreement can protect her assets, she must first get divorced. A prenuptial agreement basically is a contract that predetermines, in the event of divorce, how assets are to be split. In most cases, the parties take back what was theirs and split what they acquired jointly during the marriage.

Let's go back to our couple. Andrew doesn't have much, and very quickly will run out of funds and need to apply for Medicaid. But, the only way Sally can preserve her assets is to divorce Andrew—and you can be sure that the state is going to look very closely at that prenuptial agreement before they approve Andrew for Medicaid.

I explain all this to Sally. She loves Andrew and emotionally can't reconcile divorcing him in his time of greatest need.

"This isn't much of a choice," she observed. "Is there any alternative?"

Actually, there is. Sally can move her assets to a trust, and after five years, Andrew can qualify for Medicaid. In this way, she can spend as much of her assets for his care as she wants, but not be forced to spend it all, leaving nothing for herself to live on or to provide for her own long-term care needs.

When is the ideal time to do that? Really, Sally should have consulted an elder law attorney before or shortly after the marriage. In her case, it still isn't too late since it doesn't appear that Andrew is close to needing long-term care just yet. However, the longer she waits, the smaller that window of opportunity becomes. A little preventative medicine can go a long, long way.

Retirement Accounts—Should I Take More than the Minimum Requirement Distribution?

The fact that we are living longer than our parents and grandparents is changing many aspects of our lives. One area that will be impacted by this longevity is retirement accounts. Many of our clients have it ingrained in their minds that they must not touch their retirement accounts. They withdraw only the minimum amount each year that the government says they must—what is known as minimum required distributions. But is that really the best approach?

Retirement accounts enjoy tax-deferred status. The tax that one owes on the growth of these accounts is not paid until the money is withdrawn from the account. The thinking goes that by withdrawing the money after retirement, there will be less in taxes because the retiree will be in a lower tax bracket than during working years. Many also view their accounts as something they want to pass on as an inheritance to children and other loved ones. This combination results in the "I don't want to withdraw anything" attitude.

For many of our clients, the majority of their investments sit in retirement accounts. This makes their failure to plan for long-term care more acute because if we want to protect assets, by using trusts, for example, we must move those assets out of the retirement accounts. Doing so, however, can cause a large tax bill, one that most are reluctant to pay, thinking that they'll never really need long-term care, or they'll wait until it happens. Waiting, however, can cause disastrous results.

Moving through the twenty-first century, as a greater number of people live twenty, thirty, or even forty years in retirement, we may need to reconsider how we use our retirement accounts. Maybe it isn't best to keep the money in the account as long as possible with the specter of long-term care on the horizon. Perhaps it might be better to start withdrawing funds soon after retirement, rather than gambling that we won't need long-term care. Guessing wrong will likely result in the loss of more than just the tax on the withdrawals. Perhaps the entire account could be lost to the cost of long-term care.

As one advisor I know put it, we forget that not all the money in the account is ours. If we recognize that roughly one third of the money is Uncle Sam's, it is easier to accept the tax bill that comes with withdrawing funds. Of course, this is not a one-size-fits-all situation. Everyone needs to consider the matter individually, based on their own set of facts. But when our response to such an important decision becomes automatic, we need to go back and examine the wisdom of that approach because times are definitely changing, and we need to adjust with them.

"But Mom Won't Live to One Hundred— Or Will She?"

Quite often, when explaining long-term care planning to a family member of an aging senior, specifically when I mention the five-year Medicaid look back, the person will tell me that Mom won't live that long. Of course, no one can predict the future with any certainty so, logically, that statement is opinion and not fact and virtually useless. But it reminds me of a client I first saw a few years ago. I now retell her story frequently.

Kim's mom was already in a nursing facility when she came to see me. Mom was in spend-down mode, paying privately for nursing home care, at the rate of about $100,000 per year. She had $1.2 million in assets and minimal Social Security of $500 per month. Oh, and she was ninety-five years old.

Her situation was pretty simple and straightforward. She didn't have long-term care insurance. Her deceased husband wasn't a veteran. She didn't have any disabled children or own a home. I explained to Kim that Mom had two options, namely, private pay and Medicaid, but all assets would need to be spent first, before Medicaid eligibility could be an option, unless we did some very basic long-term care planning.

When I told Kim that we could move some assets to a trust, she asked, "But what about the Medicaid penalty and look-back period."

I explained that Mom would need to private pay for her care for five years, approximately $500,000, before we could apply for Medicaid. We discussed the likelihood of Mom living to 100. I told Kim that while I agreed that the odds were not good, she would have to evaluate that risk herself and decide if it was worthwhile to plan for that possibility. She opted not to do the planning, and thanked me.

Well, you know what happened, right? (Otherwise, I wouldn't be telling you this story.) Mom did live another five years, and Mary came back to see me when she reached 100. Mom ultimately lived to 103. We never did apply for Medicaid. But, looking at it in hindsight, had Kim made the decision to have Mom apply for Medicaid the first time we met, she would have been on Medicaid at age 100, saving approximately $360,000, the cost of care her last three years.

You might ask, "Why should Kim get this windfall? She is cheating the government." But, is that really the case? Kim now has about

$250,000, not a whole lot for someone who is on a fixed income and could live another twenty to thirty years. Kim may well find herself living in poverty, needing government handouts years before she ever needs long-term care.

The lesson to be learned is that planning isn't about predicting what is going to happen. It's like buying insurance. I buy life insurance to protect my family should I die. I am buying peace of mind, protection against a scenario that could occur. I am not "betting" on my mortality. If I don't die while the policy is in force, I won't be upset that my family didn't "collect."

It's the same thing with long-term care planning. If thoughts of nursing home care are keeping you up at night or occupying your thoughts during the day, then you ought to manage that risk. Most ninety-five-year-olds don't make it to one hundred, especially when they are at a nursing home–care level. Kim didn't think her mom would make it either. But, in the end, her mom wasn't like most ninety-five-year-olds. She beat the odds, and Kim guessed wrong!

State Pension Crisis—How Will It Affect You?

Much has been written in recent years about the health of Social Security. As the population ages, two things are happening. Fewer people are paying into the system, while at the same time more people are receiving benefits, raising concerns that the program will run out of money. But there is another, perhaps more serious, crisis developing within state employee pension programs that hasn't, until now, received as much attention. We are seeing it here in New Jersey, as are other states across the country. And it may hit some folks harder than the Social Security problem because so much more of their retirement income may be derived from a state pension than from Social Security.

As the economy remains in a funk and financial markets still struggle to recover from huge losses over the past couple of years, many pension systems have seen their investments take a big hit. Since the beginning of 2009, for example, New Jersey's pension fund has lost almost 13% in value, $10 billion to be exact. It hasn't helped that the government has taken money from the pension system to plug budget gaps in other areas in past years.

Now, our governor, Chris Christie, is assessing the situation. Will he be the one to make some hard decisions? Our last governor signed legislation raising the retirement age and barring retirement payouts for part-time employees paid less than $7,500 per year. You can be sure that other changes are coming. There have to be. There isn't enough money to pay everyone who will be entering the pension system in the next thirty years. The state has to close the gap somehow.

Now, ask yourself what you would do if the state cut your pension by 10%, 20%, or more. What would you do to replace that income? And what would you do if you were then faced with rising long-term care costs? The government is dealing with a fiscal crisis. It is reacting the same way we all do when faced with a financial crisis, tighten our belts and cut costs.

The signs are there. You just have to pay attention—and take the opportunity to protect yourself and your family. Don't assume the government will be there to protect you. It's busy trying to fix its own problems. You've got to take care of yourself. And the time to do it is now.

If We Apply for Medicaid, Have We Given Up?

When working with families struggling with the sudden realization that long-term nursing care is necessary for a loved one, two issues quite often cause internal conflict. One is the fear that, at $8,000 to $10,000 a month or more, "We're going to run out of money." The other is the desire to do everything possible to bring their loved one home. In other words, by applying for nursing home Medicaid, does that mean we're giving up on going home?

The answer is "absolutely not." As the cost of long-term care increases and the population continues to age, two things become increasingly clear. It is usually less expensive to receive long-term care at home, and most people prefer to receive their care at home. Yet, when 24/7 care is necessary and you've run out of money, getting Medicaid to cover care at home has always been much harder than in a nursing home. But that is starting to change.

Many states have several community waiver programs. That's what Medicaid calls programs that pay for long-term care outside of a nursing home, in the community. It could be in a person's own home or in an assisted-living facility. In New Jersey, for example, a law was enacted in 2006 to enable Medicaid nursing home residents to return to the community provided they are medically able to do so. In 2009, the law was expanded to include several waiver programs.

So, what does this mean in plain English? It means that if someone's spouse is in a nursing home on Medicaid, he or she doesn't have to stay there. We must contact the nursing home social worker, who will then assemble a team of nursing home staff and the resident's family, who will discuss whether and how that can be done while preserving the health and safety of the resident.

The financial eligibility requirements for many waiver programs are similar to those for institutional (nursing home) Medicaid, but in some cases there are also significant differences. However, these programs can be a great option for many families struggling with the need for nursing home care now but who don't want to give up on the possibility of bringing their loved one home at some point down the road.

Chapter 6

Estate Planning

Why Do I Need a Will?

Individuals work a lifetime at accumulating assets, personal property, and mementos. It only takes a little time to make sure those valued items pass on to your loved ones. If executed correctly, a last will and testament can clearly state your wishes and ensure they are carried out. Other reasons to take the time to prepare a will are the following:

1. You care about your family and loved ones, so you do not want to leave them to figure everything out on their own after your death. By planning, you are conveying the message they are important enough for you to have taken the time to state what your wishes are with respect to your property and assets.

2. People may not die in the order you plan, so if a joint account owner passes away before you do, you have a contingency plan in place. Your family and loved ones will know what your wishes are if the co-owners on your accounts die before you do.

3. You want to include plans for a bequest or gift to a charitable, religious, social, or community organization that has played a significant role in your life or the life of a loved one. It is important to take the time to include them in your planning.

4. You do not want the state to determine how your assets and property are divided and distributed. The state will divide that property between your spouse and children or other relatives. You want to make that decision yourself, rather than having the state decide who inherits your property by certain inflexible and impersonal state laws, some of which may be counter to your personal wishes.

5. You do not want your family to fight over important personal items. It is easier to make a decision and communicate your wishes to your loved ones.

6. You do not want a court to determine who is to be your executor and take care of your affairs after your death. A court may insist that a bond be posted, which will cost the estate several thousand dollars or more. A will can state that no bond is necessary.

7. A will can be changed. Therefore, if circumstances change, you have the ability to make whatever changes you deem appropriate. Those circumstances may be due to the death of family members or named executors, or changes in your financial situation or tax laws.

8. You do not want your estate to pay estate taxes. Through proper planning, federal and state estate taxes can be minimized or avoided altogether.

The Dangers of an
Improperly Drafted Will

A number of years ago, I received a call from a potential client who had the following tale to tell. Denise's husband, Jason, had died, leaving a will and some assets, one of which was a 401(k) retirement plan. The marriage was the second for Jason, who had two sons from his first marriage. While he was single, he had changed the beneficiaries of his life insurance and 401(k) plan to his sons and had redone his will.

Jason and Denise bought a new home together. They asked their real estate attorney, who handled the purchase for them, to draft new wills as well. Jason listed for his attorney the assets he wanted to pass to his sons, and those to Denise. The 401(k) he wanted to leave to Denise. Unfortunately, the attorney didn't understand the difference between probate and nonprobate assets. So when he wrote a will that specifically left the 401(k) to Denise, he didn't know that the will had no effect on this asset because the beneficiary designations on file for the 401(k) plan still listed Jason's sons.

When Jason died, Denise received a big shock when she was told that she had no interest in the $500,000 401(k). That's because a will doesn't automatically control the distribution of all your assets. Contract property such as life insurance, annuities, and retirement accounts pass in accordance with whom you have designated on the beneficiary forms completed and filed with the life insurance and annuity companies or retirement account custodians. Other types of property pass by operation of law such as joint accounts with right of survivorship or real estate that is owned by husband and wife. When one owner dies, the property automatically passes to the surviving owner. It does not matter what the will says.

That is what happened in our story. The 401(k) is contract property, so it passed according to the beneficiary designation form on file, not by the will. Denise tried unsuccessfully to get a court order directing the funds be paid to her. She did recover about half of the account balance, filing a malpractice action against the attorney who drafted Jason's will, for failing to recognize that listing the 401(k) account in the will was meaningless.

The moral of the story is that, although many people think drafting a will is simple, and often undertake to do it themselves or ask the attorney who did other work for them to handle this task as well, they may miss important steps that must be taken, and that can lead to a lot of heartache and loss of money.

When Can an Alternate Executor Take Over?

Very often, when I prepare wills, powers of attorney, and health-care directives (living wills) for clients, they react with surprise when they see the length of my documents.

"Why," they say, "is the will you are preparing twenty-plus pages when my previous one was only two?"

"The document is designed to cover as many scenarios as possible," I explain, "not knowing which scenario may in fact occur." It is not good enough to simply address the most likely ones, especially if yours turns out to be one of the uncommon ones.

Narrowly or poorly drafted wills can cause unpleasant and expensive results. Let's take the simple task of designating an executor, the person who is appointed the official representative of the estate and is charged with gathering the assets, paying the debts and taxes, if any, following the instructions set forth in the will, and making final distributions to the heirs. It is a good idea to have one or more backup or alternate executors, in case someone can't or won't serve, when the time comes.

Now, most people would think in terms of the executor dying as the reason a backup is necessary, but that is just one possible scenario. Yet, I frequently see a will drawn up that states, "If my executor dies then I appoint my alternate to serve."

Let's say Child A is the executor and Child B is the alternate. Mom dies, and A doesn't want to serve. No problem. Child A will step aside in favor of Child B, right? Except that Child A is alive and the will only provides that Child B can serve if Child A has died. So, what now?

Child B can serve as administrator. Same role and responsibilities, but some very important differences. An executor can serve without a bond if the will so provides, but an administrator cannot. And that can be an expensive difference. The bond acts similar to an insurance policy in that the company issuing the bond will pay out the inheritance if the assets are lost or misappropriated. The bigger the estate is, the higher the cost—sometimes tens of thousands of dollars. Although a bond can be very important, many close-knit families see it as unnecessary. Unfortunately, in our case there is no choice. Had the will specifically stated that the alternate can step in if the executor dies or otherwise can't or won't serve, then the bond could have been avoided. This can be a very expensive mistake, and a reason you want to be sure that the attorney drafting your will is experienced in estate planning or elder law.

If We Move to a New State, Do I Need a New Will?

People often ask whether there is a need to change their wills when they move to another state. Although a will made in one state doesn't become invalid in another, the laws in the new state may make certain provisions of your will invalid. It is a good idea to check with a lawyer in your new state. For example, property laws vary from state to state. Some states are what we call "community property" states. Property acquired during marriage is considered community property and gives certain rights to the spouse. Arizona, California, Idaho, New Mexico, Louisiana, Washington, Nevada, Texas, Wisconsin, and Alaska are community property states. The other states are common law states, where married couples can own property individually.

This has implications for the transfer of assets upon death. Additionally, states may vary as to what assets pass automatically to surviving co-owners and which pass by way of a will. There may also be specific language you will want to place in your will that will make probating easier. Finally, your health-care directive and power of attorney should be considered in light of any specific requirements in your new state. Oftentimes, an out-of-state power of attorney, while still valid, may be questioned by a financial institution just because it is not in the form they are accustomed to. Sometimes it is just easier to execute a new document that does conform with that state's laws.

Living Trusts

There has been a deluge of advertising and publicity in recent years on the benefits of living trusts. Living trusts are estate planning devices designed to eliminate the need to probate an individual's estate at his/her death. Very often, my clients ask me if such a trust is right for them.

Although probate avoidance can be a worthwhile objective, it is not a relevant or important consideration in many cases. In states such as California or New York, where probate can be expensive and time consuming, living trusts are more advantageous. Other states, however, such as New Jersey, are "probate-friendly" states. In most cases, probate filing fees are no more than a few hundred dollars. In probate-friendly states, unless the validity of a will is challenged, which is rare, the court does not oversee the administration of the estate. Only where there is a dispute does a judge usually get involved, and that is where probate becomes costly. Keep in mind that the same dispute can arise in connection with a living trust, leading to the same court intervention and cost.

Another important point to remember is that all your assets must be held in the trust at the time of your death. If not, then your heirs will need to go through the probate process anyway, to distribute those assets held outside the trust. We often see, especially as time passes, that people forget that they need to keep assets in the trust, so that a substantial portion are outside the trust, making probate necessary anyway.

Living trusts are often advertised as insuring privacy concerning details of your finances, whereas probate does not. This is simply not true. Although it is true that anyone can obtain a copy of your will from the surrogate once it is admitted to probate, in most states there is no disclosure of financial details, either in the will or as part of the routine probate process. In fact, in most cases, no formal accounting is required. Again, only if there is a will contest or other dispute does disclosure become necessary.

Perhaps most importantly, most living trusts will not protect assets from being countable and spent down for nursing home care before qualifying for Medicaid benefits. Only carefully drafted Medicaid-planning trusts will protect assets, and making provisions for the payment of nursing home care during the period of the resulting Medicaid transfer penalty must be considered.

So, when is a living trust suitable? When an individual has property that is subject to probate in more than one state. For example, if you own real estate in three different states, your executor may have to go through the probate process in each state in order to distribute that property. A living trust can avoid that hassle and expense. But you should always consider the Medicaid and asset-protection implications.

The bottom line when it comes to living trusts is to get proper advice before jumping into one. Or perhaps even better still, seek the advice of a qualified elder law attorney, who can discuss every option with you. A living trust may meet your particular needs. But then again, it may not.

How Long-Term Care
Can Destroy an Estate Plan

Whenever we meet with new clients, especially married ones, I always want to review the estate-planning documents that they currently have. Sometimes those documents are ten, twenty, or thirty years old.

Other times, the clients will say, "Oh, we just had our wills updated in the last year, so we're good there." Yet, when I review the documents, I find that they are not suitable for their current needs. How can this be?

Very simply, no one considered how long-term care costs can completely destroy an estate plan. When one spouse needs nursing home care and the other does not, a spend-down of assets must occur. The healthy spouse gets to keep half of the couple's assets up to a current maximum of $109,540 and a home, if he or she is living there. The ill spouse can then get Medicaid. But what happens if the healthy spouse dies first?

Well, in most cases the will provides that everything is left to the surviving spouse, and then to the children after the surviving spouse dies. Or, perhaps, the will establishes a bypass trust for the surviving spouse, to save on estate taxes. In either case, the assets will now be accessible to the surviving spouse, who, in our examples, is on Medicaid. One of two things will happen. Either the assets must be given to the state to pay back Medicaid benefits received and the surviving spouse can continue to receive benefits, or the alternative is to terminate Medicaid and begin private paying for care until all the assets are spent and then reapply for Medicaid.

Neither scenario is very appealing and need not happen if we modify the will. Instead of leaving everything to the ill spouse, we leave the assets to a trust for that spouse, but—and here is the key—a trust whose assets don't count for Medicaid eligibility purposes. Now, those assets are available to be used for other needs not covered by Medicaid. And when the surviving spouse passes away, there will likely be something left to pass on to the next generation, an important goal for many families.

Does this mean that everyone should set up their will in this manner and that leaving everything to your spouse is the wrong thing to do? Not necessarily. What I am saying is that you do need to sit down with an elder law attorney who is well versed in the long-term care system. You may have a will that was suitable for your needs at the time it was created, but things change and your plan may need to be changed too. You may be leaving yourself vulnerable. The state says you have to spend down most of your assets toward long-term care. With a poorly drafted estate plan, you may end up spending all of your assets toward care, something even the state doesn't require you to do.

What Michael Jackson and Yung-Ching Wang Can Teach Us All

The deaths of two wealthy men, one very well known, the other not, illustrates yet again the complications and costs of not preparing an estate plan. The first is the story about Michael Jackson's death and its aftermath. No doubt we will be bombarded with this story for years to come. Jackson left a mountain of debt, assets that in death are probably worth more than when he was alive, and a less-than-traditional family. Jackson did, however, do some things right. He left a will that included trusts for his children and a clear indication of who he wished to be appointed as their guardian.

Then there is Yung-Ching Wang. Most people probably never heard of Wang, but when he died in 2008 at the age of ninety-one, he was one of the wealthiest people in the world. Wang was a true success story. Born into poverty, the son of Taiwanese farmers, he turned a $700,000 loan from the United States government during the height of the Cold War into a multibillion-dollar international manufacturing conglomerate. His company, Formosa Plastics, became the largest manufacturer of the ubiquitous plastic materials that we find in all kinds of products today.

By all accounts, Wang was a management guru and a visionary. His personal life was a little bit more, shall we say, messy. He left a wife, to whom he was married for seventy-two years, and nine children. None of those children, however, were born to his wife. Oh, and he didn't have a will. No written plan of distribution from a man whose rightful heirs are now open to interpretation and who left property and other assets around the United States and around the world.

One of his sons has filed a complaint in New Jersey state court (Wang was a part-time resident in New Jersey) seeking to be appointed administrator, i.e., the official estate representative charged with gathering assets, paying all debts and taxes, and distributing the balance to the heirs. He has a fight on his hands from two of his sisters. Had Wang executed a will appointing someone, this initial fight could have been avoided.

The battle promises to last for years and drain the estate of countless dollars. One of the big questions is who the rightful heirs should be, not an easy answer since Wang fathered his children with several different women. New Jersey's intestacy laws address distribution of estates when

108

no valid will exists, but the laws are not perfect and there no doubt will be issues for which clear-cut answers don't exist. Legal battles will ensue.

The lessons learned from the Michael Jackson and Yung-Ching Wang cases should be clear to all of us. You can save your family much heartache and expense by leaving a clearly thought-out estate plan. In Jackson's and Wang's cases, their estates are so complicated that courts will need to step in at some point to assist in the distribution. However, Jackson's family will have a much easier time than Wang's, because Jackson at least took care to express his wishes in writing. For the average estate, that usually is enough to eliminate the fighting that typically ensues when a loved one passes away.

New Estate Tax Law in 2011

Unlike the end of 2009, when Congress tried to pass a law preventing the no estate tax in 2010 scenario, in late 2010, it did manage to pass a law extending the Bush era tax cuts that went into effect in 2002 but were set to expire on December 31, 2010. So, what does that mean for 2011 and beyond?

Well, first of all, the new law is yet another temporary solution, this time for two years. So, we might be right back here again in December 2012. Nevertheless, the changes come as a bit of a surprise. To review, had there been no change, the federal estate tax would have returned in 2011 for estates greater than $1,000,000, with a tax rate of 55%. There had been some talk about going back to an exemption amount of $3,500,000, which was the case in 2009. Instead, President Obama signed into law an exemption amount of $5,000,000 and a tax rate of 35%.

For a married couple with some tax planning, that means they can transfer as much as $10,000,000 without paying federal estate tax. Not bad. Keep in mind, however, that many states have their own estate tax, which remains unaffected by this new law. New Jersey residents, for example, owe tax on estates greater than $675,000, and New York residents on estates greater than $1,000,000.

What is somewhat surprising, however, is that the federal gift tax exclusion is once again unified with the estate tax. Over the last nine years, as the federal estate tax exemption kept increasing, the lifetime gift exclusion remained at $1,000,000. In 2011, however, the gift tax exclusion increased to $5,000,000. The gift tax rate will be 35%, the same as the estate tax rate.

So, what does this all mean for you and me? First, most estates will escape federal estate tax, but estate planning will still be necessary to minimize or, in some cases, completely avoid state estate taxes. Secondly, there are significant reasons to consider gifting more than the $13,000 per person per year annual gifts, now that $5,000,000 of gifts are exempt. It might be a good idea to take advantage of the huge gift exclusion, which may or may not be available beyond 2012. What remains unchanged, however, is the specter of long-term care. Before one considers any gifting, a carefully crafted long-term care plan must be in place.

I Don't Have an Estate
Tax Problem—Do I?

For the past ten years, it seems, the federal estate tax laws have been in a constant state of change. At the end of 2010, Congress set the federal exemption, that amount of assets that is free of federal estate tax, at $5,000,000 for the years 2011 and 2012. For this reason, when people call our office to discuss estate planning, they will often begin by saying that they are not concerned about estate tax. I have to correct them, however, because most states have their own estate tax, which may kick in on smaller estates where the federal tax isn't a concern. So, how big might such an estate tax bill be?

First, here's a little background. Under previous laws, Congress permitted a dollar-for-dollar credit toward the federal estate tax for any state estate and inheritance taxes paid up to a certain limit. So, many states established their estate tax structures to "soak up" the maximum credit that Congress permitted. In essence, the federal government shared a portion of its tax revenue with the states. When it raised the federal exemption, however, Congress decided it could no longer share a smaller tax revenue with the states; so it phased out this credit. Many states, in response, changed their tax laws to preserve their revenue stream. New Jersey now has an estate tax that kicks in on estates greater than $675,000, and New York on estates greater than $1,000,000.

New Jersey's estate tax starts out at 4.8% and gradually increases to a maximum of 16%. New York's estate tax also maxes out at 16%. As I explain to our clients, we usually see federal estate taxes in the six- to seven-figure range, and state estate taxes in the tens of thousands of dollars on the low end and hundreds of thousands of dollars on the higher end.

What can you do to reduce, or even eliminate, this tax? Well, for starters, in the case of married couples, a bypass or credit shelter trust should be employed. This will save substantial amounts of tax that would be paid by your children at the death of the second parent to die. But you must have this trust set forth in your will before you pass away.

What if it's too late for that? Purchasing life insurance to pay the tax is another solution, which may be especially desirable where the estate consists of real estate that the family doesn't want to sell just to pay the tax. And, incidentally, placing that insurance in a life insurance trust is usually a good idea. Otherwise, you end up paying estate tax on the life insurance that you bought to pay the tax in the first place.

Chapter 7

Estate Administration

What to Do When a Loved One Dies

After a loved one dies, a number of legal and financial affairs must be addressed. The following is a list of issues to consider.

1. The funeral home should provide certified copies of the death certificate. The number of copies needed depends on the assets remaining at the time of death.

2. The funeral home should contact the Social Security Administration to report the death. The surviving spouse, if any, is entitled to a one-time death benefit of approximately $250. In addition, he/she may begin receiving the deceased spouse's monthly Social Security payment if it was higher.

3. The death must be reported to all life insurance companies, who will then send a claim form to complete and return with a certified copy of the death certificate. The death benefit proceeds will then be issued to the beneficiaries. (Retirement plans, such as IRAs and annuities, work much the same way. Contact the appropriate company, complete the necessary claim forms, and submit a death certificate before the proceeds will be distributed to the beneficiaries.)

4. Contact the VA and/or any former employer to report the death. A surviving spouse may be entitled to a death benefit or a monthly survivor's pension check.

5. If your loved one owned real estate in joint tenancy with another individual, a new deed should be prepared, removing the deceased owner's name from the title. (Keep in mind that if the home is now vacant, there will most likely be a limit on how long the home will continue to be insured—check with the insurance company.)

6. For any car owned jointly with another individual or to be distributed to a designated beneficiary, the title papers and death certificate or surrogate certificate should be filed with the Department of Motor Vehicles so a new title may be issued.

7. Other assets such as bank accounts, CDs, stocks, and bonds should be handled similarly to real estate and vehicles. Assets with payable on death (POD) or transfer on death (TOD) designations will require that a death certificate be provided to the appropriate financial institution.

Finally, you may be wondering if probate of the will is necessary. Typically, only if there are assets titled in your loved one's name alone with no beneficiary designation at the time of death will probate of the will be necessary. If there is no will, then the probate court must appoint an administrator and state law will determine the distribution of the assets. (There is sometimes a simplified process if the assets remaining at the time of death are relatively minimal.)

Regardless of the amount of assets and how they are titled, it is always wise to contact an elder law attorney for guidance after the loss of a loved one.

Failing to Probate in a Timely Manner

Many times when we get a call from a family member whose loved one has died, the caller is thinking that the death triggers all kinds of required action with short time lines. Although there are some deadlines to be concerned about (i.e., taxes), what people don't realize is that there is no deadline to probating a will or administering an estate.

This can cause problems however. A common scenario we see is where a homeowner dies but other family members continue to live in the home. The government isn't going to remind you that there may be taxes to pay and that assets need to be transferred from the deceased person to heirs. Typically, life goes on, and so long as the real estate taxes and other bills associated with maintaining the property are paid, everything seems OK. We had a case come to our office that illustrates the problem.

Jane called us because she lived in a home that she owned (or so she thought). She wanted to take a home equity loan so she could do some renovations. When the bank's title company conducted a title search, she learned that, in fact, she only held title to half of the house. She said her Aunt Sarah had transferred the other half to her (Sarah died ten years earlier), but that was never done, as it turned out. So, Sarah and Jane co-owned the house, but as tenants in common, not with right of survivorship.

When Sarah died, Jane did not, by operation of law, inherit Sarah's 50%. Instead, Sarah's interest would pass according to her will. Except that Jane had no idea where the will was or if there ever was a will. Sarah's interest would then pass under New Jersey's intestacy laws, that set of laws that determines how property passes when the deceased person left no will. Sarah had no other known family members, so it appeared that Jane, as the niece, would inherit. But hold on a second. It turns out that "Aunt Sarah" wasn't really Jane's aunt. She was "like an aunt" to her, but there was no family relation at all.

So, who then was entitled to Sarah's 50%? Believe or not, under the intestacy laws, the State of New Jersey. If Jane wanted the house, she'd have to buy it back from the state. And that's exactly what she did. First, we had to file a legal action asking a judge to appoint an administrator for Sarah's estate. We then had to negotiate a purchase price. Jane did get some credit for paying taxes and insurance on the home reduced by the value of her right to occupy 100% of a home of which she only owned half. She was able to get her home equity loan and fix up the property, but she had to pay the state over $100,000 first, and the whole process to straighten out the mess took over a year.

Again, here was a situation that was completely avoidable. Stated intentions while Sarah was alive should have been carried through on paper. Additionally, when Sarah died, her estate needed to be administered. The passing of ten years only served to make things more complicated.

How to Turn a Simple Estate Matter into a Complex Mess

There are many misconceptions about estate administration and probate. So often when someone asks me about it, they'll typically tell me that their family member's estate matter is not that complicated, that they can handle it themselves. The following is a cautionary tale for the do-it-yourselfer.

Maggie died without a will. She never married, and had no children. She did have three sisters, Joan, Ann, and Betsy. Betsy had died before Maggie, leaving two children, Jim and John. Joan was appointed administrator of Maggie's estate and thought she could handle things herself. However, she made two big mistakes.

Under intestacy laws, Maggie's sisters were entitled to split her estate three ways. That's where Joan made her first mistake. A family friend told her she should split the estate two ways, not three, because, since Betsy had died, she wasn't entitled to receive anything. Except that under New Jersey's intestacy laws, Betsy's share should have passed to Jim and John.

Then, Joan made her second mistake. New Jersey has an inheritance tax payable based on the relationship of the heir to the decedent (the person who died). Siblings are Class C beneficiaries. Nephews are Class D beneficiaries. Each class has a different tax rate. So, when Joan filed the inheritance tax return indicating that she and Ann were the heirs, she didn't pay enough tax.

When Jim and John realized they were entitled to receive a share of Maggie's estate, they contacted an attorney who then contacted Joan. Joan had already distributed the estate assets, filed the tax return, and paid the tax by the eight-month deadline. So, now she has a problem. Joan has to retrieve funds from Ann to then pay Jim and John their proper share. She also must file an amended tax return with the state and pay the proper amount of tax, as well as a penalty for late payment at 10% per year.

The irony of the story is that the estate was a simple one, with a few bank accounts to be administered and an uncomplicated tax return. But by trying to do it herself, Maggie made mistakes that an experienced estate attorney would have recognized right away. So now it will be more complicated to fix things. A lesson learned the hard way.

How Harriet's Estate Plan
Destroyed Her Family

If I have a will, does it mean my wishes will be carried out and my property will be distributed exactly according to my instructions? Not necessarily. That's because not all property is probate property, automatically passed by way of a will. And when things don't work out the way everyone expected them to, it leads to anger, hurt feelings, and the breakup of families. Take the case of Harriet.

Harriet had two children from a first marriage. Her first husband died when her children were young. She married for a second time to Ozzie. Ozzie and Harriet were married for twenty years and, by all accounts, Ozzie's relationship with Harriet's children was great. Harriet had gone to great lengths to set out a plan of distributing assets among her children and Ozzie, and making that plan known to all. A large part of her assets were held in one investment account, which was worth $500,000. She told her attorney who drafted her will that she wished to leave 50% of the account to her two children, and the other 50% to Ozzie.

Harriet's attorney prepared her will exactly according to her instructtions, with a paragraph identifying the investment account and how it was to be distributed. But the attorney cautioned Harriet that the account needed to remain in her name alone. He told her not to put another owner on the account and not to name beneficiaries upon her death. That's because doing either would override the will.

Well, you can imagine what happened. Harriet died several years later. She didn't change her will, but when her children sat down with Ozzie they got the shock of their life when they learned that the account was no longer just in Harriet's name. It was now a joint account with right of survivorship. That means Ozzie is entitled to 100% of the account, and Harriet's kids get nothing, unless Ozzie decides to honor Harriet's wishes.

Of course, that's if it still was Harriet's wish to split the account 50/50. Maybe it was, maybe it wasn't. Only Harriet could say for sure, and of course she could no longer say. The children suspected that Ozzie had Harriet change the account, although Ozzie swears that wasn't the case, that he doesn't even recall when she made the change. Imagine how uncomfortable the family situation is now. The children are talking about filing suit, and Ozzie doesn't know what to do.

This is another example of how poor planning can really destroy family harmony and cause a whole lot of pain.

Why Edna's Estate Plan Is
No Better Than Harriet's

We were just discussing how Harriet's estate plan actually destroyed family harmony. Now, I'll share with you Edna's mistake; one that I see so often. Edna has three children, all of whom she loves equally. She came to see me because she wanted to discuss her will. She owns a home and investments totaling approximately $450,000. Edna explained that she wants to leave her house (or really the proceeds from the sale after her death) to her children equally.

I then asked about the rest of her assets and she said, "Don't worry, I've taken care of it."

I asked her how she had done that, and she replied that she has her investments in laddered CDs naming each of her children as the POD beneficiary on a third of the total investment. In this way, each child will receive $150,000 when she dies. I then posed to her a number of scenarios under which that wouldn't happen, meaning there could very well be an uneven distribution, leading to the same problem that Harriet's family experienced.

Edna has made a common mistake I see frequently. She assumes that the amount of money she has and where she has it will remain unchanged. That is very unlikely. For example, when a CD matures she may roll it over to a new one or she may decide not to, either because she needs the money to live on or because she has decided to invest it elsewhere. So, what happens if the money is sitting in her checking account when she dies and that CD happened to be money that would have passed to her son, Bob? Well, Bob won't receive that money unless he was a co-owner of the checking account. He'll receive less than his siblings. In fact, if his sister, Terry, becomes a co-owner, because she lives nearby and pays Edna's bills, then Terry will receive "Bob's share." Now, you might say that Terry can just give that money to Bob if everyone agrees that this is what Mom wanted. Yes, that's true, but it assumes that everyone is aware and agrees on what Edna wanted. It also requires Terry to make a gift to Bob that may result in gift tax consequences for her.

A bigger concern is long-term care, of which Edna is completely unaware. As she ages, she may need assistance at home, in an assisted-living facility, or even a nursing home. If so, and she has done no planning for it, then she will need to spend down huge chunks of assets toward that care. Again, that will completely destroy her nice neat division into three. As each CD comes due and she spends it, her estate plan becomes unbalanced. And if Terry is managing Edna's care and happens to take one of "Bob's or brother Joe's" CDs, that's a sure way to destroy family harmony. And that's clearly the last thing that Edna wants.

Again, estate and long-term care planning with the help of a trusted elder law attorney will prevent these types of situations that could occur when we think we can go it alone on such involved and crucial matters.

We Don't Owe Any Estate Tax, So What the Heck Is Inheritance Tax?

I got a call from Tom last week. His brother Tim died five months ago. Tim had never married, and had no children, leaving his estate of assets totaling $150,000 to Tom. Everything seemed so simple. There was no need to pay taxes, or so he thought, because there is no federal estate tax in 2010 and New Jersey estate tax is only owed on estates greater than $675,000. So, why was Tom's friend telling him he may have to pay taxes?

What Tom's friend was talking about is inheritance tax. Only a handful of states have it, and New Jersey is one of them. Inheritance tax works differently from estate tax, which is based on the size of the estate. Inheritance tax, on the other hand, is based on the relationship of the heirs to the decedent (person who died). In New Jersey, parents, grandparents, children, grandchildren, spouses, and domestic partners are exempt from the tax. So are stepchildren, but not step-grandchildren. Siblings, sons-in-law, and daughters-in-law pay tax at one rate, and other more distant relatives and nonrelatives pay tax at another rate.

Inheritance tax is due eight months after death, one month before the estate tax is due. In cases where both estate and inheritance tax are due, the total combined tax is not greater than the larger of the two taxes. In essence, if inheritance tax is due, then that payment acts as a credit toward the estate tax.

Tom, like most people, was unaware of inheritance tax. It is typically owed on estates where there are no spouses or children. In his case, the tax totals about $13,000, and if not paid, carries a 10% per year interest rate. There are other quirks in terms of what is taxed and what isn't. For example, life insurance isn't subject to the tax if you've left it to named beneficiaries. However, if those people have all died, and the insurance is left to the estate, then it is taxed. Life insurance is subject to estate tax. It is easy to get tripped up by which assets are taxed for inheritance, and which for estate tax purposes.

The point is that each estate has to be looked at individually. Just because your friend or neighbor didn't have to pay inheritance tax doesn't mean you don't have to. I explained to Tom that we still have time to complete the return and pay the tax on time. The last thing he wants is the state coming after him for unpaid tax.

Chapter 8

Powers of Attorney, Health-Care Directives, and Guardianships

What Happens if My Bank Refuses to Honor My Power of Attorney?

As I often tell clients, one of the most important documents that everyone should have is a power of attorney. A power of attorney allows you to designate someone to conduct financial and other transactions on your behalf. The ease with which anyone can execute such a document is a positive, but can also be a negative because of the risk of it being abused. And therein lies the problem when it comes to being accepted by a third party, such as a financial institution or bank.

When we prepare a power of attorney for a client, we draft it with the client's needs in mind as well as the mind-set that we may not have another opportunity to redo it later. Therefore, it must be as broad as necessary to cover all possible scenarios in which it may be used by the agent. We also tell clients that when their agent presents the document to a bank or other financial institution, the first reaction may be that the bank will want our client (the "principal," that is, the person signing the power of attorney in favor of the "agent") to execute another power of attorney on their own form.

The bank's reason is usually a concern about liability, i.e., being sued for honoring an invalid power of attorney. However, the law provides a measure of protection for both the principal and the bank. New Jersey law states that a bank must accept a power of attorney that conforms to the law unless the principal's signature is not genuine or the bank has actual notice that the principal has died, the power of attorney has been revoked, or the principal was under a disability when the document was signed, meaning he/she wasn't competent to sign it.

The problem presented to clients is that the bank employee is usually following bank policy set by their legal department, that they want the principal to sign their own document, typically in front of one of their own employees. Obviously, this makes it easier for them to be sure the document is valid, but it frustrates the purpose and benefit of the law, that the principal can sign one document to cover all scenarios. Persistence with the bank employee and sometimes intervention by the elder law attorney will usually overcome this resistance and convince the bank to honor a valid power of attorney.

It helps to know a little bit about the law because the person you are dealing with at the bank probably doesn't and will tell you they are simply "following bank policy." This policy, however, is simply the easy way out for the financial institution. But it is not at all helpful to the client, especially in situations in which physical frailties prevent him or her from physically appearing at each bank to execute a separate power of attorney. There is certainly a risk of abuse of a power of attorney by an agent, and banks should be vigilant in protecting against such fraud. However, a blanket refusal to honor any power of attorney that is not on "their" form goes too far and frustrates many people's intent.

Health-Care Directives—The Right to Make Medical Decisions

The legal battle over Terri Schiavo several years ago captured the nation's attention. The Florida woman's family fought fifteen years over her right to die because she left no living will. How can you avoid the same situation? Some common questions and answers follow. Keep in mind that you should consult with an attorney in your state since the laws do vary.

What is a health-care directive (HCD)? Every state recognizes the fundamental right to make voluntary, informed choices about medical care. If you lose decision-making capacity and can no longer participate actively in making health-care decisions, the law says you can plan ahead with a written HCD.

When and how can I prepare one? You can sign an HCD at any time provided you are competent to do so. It must be in writing, and signed and dated in front of an attorney, notary public, or two witnesses, depending on state law.

When does the HCD become effective? When you give it to a medical provider and a doctor decides that you lack capacity to make a medical decision.

What can I place in an HCD? You may appoint another person (agent) to make medical decisions for you. This is called a proxy directive. You may direct the agent to consult with others, such as family and friends, before making medical decisions.

You may also sign a document that states your general philosophy and objectives or wishes regarding treatment, including specific instructions as to the types of treatment or care to be provided or withheld. This is an instruction directive (commonly known as a **living will**).

A third type of directive is one that both designates an agent and has specific instructions regarding treatment.

Must a hospital or doctor honor an HCD? The laws in your state may permit private, religiously affiliated health-care institutions to develop policies and practices as to when they will decline to participate in withholding measures to sustain life. This policy must be written and given to patients and their families. It is a good practice to discuss with your doctors whether they would object to honoring your wishes and to find out the policy at the local hospital where you would most likely be admitted.

Is there anything else I should know? It is a good idea to specifically authorize the release of medical information to your agent under the federal HIPAA privacy laws. Without it, your doctors may refuse to release information to your agent that he/she needs to make an informed decision.

What should I do next? Many hospitals have HCD forms that patients may complete. These forms are generic in nature and may or may not be suitable for you. You can also consult an elder law or estate planning attorney, who can tailor an HCD to your particular wants and needs.

Understanding Life-Sustaining Measures

You decide to follow your physician's and attorney's advice and complete your health-care directive, thus providing a clear understanding of your wishes as they relate to life-sustaining measures. Do you want medical treatment in an "end-of-life" situation? But what exactly does "life sustaining" mean?

Life-sustaining measures can be defined as any medical treatment in which the primary goal is to prolong life rather than treat the underlying condition. In such cases, an individual's own body is not capable of sustaining proper functioning on its own without medical intervention.

Artificial nutrition and hydration are utilized when one is not receiving the nutrients necessary for health and well-being. Artificial nutrition (tube feeding) requires a tube be placed into the stomach or the upper intestine. Hydration (fluid replacement) involves tube placement intravenously (IV) via a needle.

Cardiopulmonary resuscitation (CPR) is used when an individual's heartbeat and/or breathing has stopped. CPR includes treatments such as mouth-to-mouth resuscitation, chest compressions, electric shock, and/or drugs to restart the heart. CPR can be life saving; however, there is a risk of broken or cracked ribs, punctured lungs, and death.

Mechanical ventilation supports a person's breathing when they can no longer breathe on their own. In this situation, a ventilator forces air into the lungs via tubing in the mouth or nose.

Dialysis is the artificial process by which waste products and excess water are removed from the blood, when the kidneys are no longer able to do so.

These examples of life-sustaining treatments are just a few of the more common measures taken when one or more body systems are not working properly. Deciding what, if any, treatments are right for you should depend on several factors.

Does the treatment relieve suffering, restore functioning, or enhance the quality of life? If so, these would be some of the benefits of treatment. Conversely, a treatment may be considered problematic if it is painful, prolongs the dying process, or negatively affects the quality of life. Other questions to ask yourself might be: What are my values as they relate to life prolonging measures? Who will carry out my wishes if I become incapacitated? If I start treatment and it does not improve my status, will I want to continue treatment? If so, when? (It should be noted that it is ethically and legally acceptable to discontinue treatment that is no longer of benefit. The disease, and not the withdrawal of treatment, causes death.)

How you choose to complete your health-care directive and what measures you choose to take are up to you. Talk to your doctor and attorney, and don't be afraid to ask questions if you don't understand something. Ultimately, understanding your health-care directive and the medical terminology associated with it will enable you to communicate your wishes to those providing your health-care and increase the likelihood that your wishes will be honored.

Guardianship as a Substitute for Poor Planning

Sometimes we get a call concerning an elderly parent or other family member who doesn't have a financial power of attorney or health-care power of attorney. A financial power of attorney is a document that appoints someone to carry out financial and other nonmedical transactions and decisions. This could be paying bills, writing checks, speaking with credit card companies, etc. A health-care power of attorney designates someone to make medical decisions for you if you cannot make them yourself. The law provides a relatively inexpensive and easy way to make these designations, but they must be in writing and executed in the proper manner.

Problems typically arise when these documents aren't in place, and it's too late to sign them, meaning the person is no longer competent to do so. The only alternative is guardianship. A guardian is a court-appointed person, usually a family member if one is suitable and willing to serve, who acts in a fiduciary capacity on behalf of the incapacitated individual. More often than not, a guardian becomes necessary because of lack of planning. This can have devastating ramifications. An example can help illustrate.

Lou had a stroke. He has no power of attorney or health-care directive. Gina, his wife, can't access accounts in Lou's name alone. Lou needs nursing home care, and bills must be paid. Gina wants to qualify Lou for Medicaid and protect as much as she can for herself. This may involve moving or retitling assets, such as the marital home. Except that without the power of attorney, she can't do anything. So, now she must file a petition in court, asking a judge to appoint her guardian for Lou.

First, she'll need two doctors to examine him and file reports. She must advise the court of all the couple's assets. Then, the court will need to assign an attorney to represent and meet with Lou and report back to the judge. Gina will have to appear before the judge before she will be appointed, and then she probably will have to post a bond, similar to an insurance policy, based on the amount of assets she will be entrusted with. Of course, these are her assets too, but she'll need to report back to the court periodically to explain what she is doing.

The end result is that what was a private matter among family is now a very public matter overseen by a court system that will have the final say on what is done and why.

Mom Needs Help but Won't Accept It—Can We Apply for Guardianship?

The caller gives me the following fact pattern or some variation. Mom's health is deteriorating. Her behavior is becoming extremely erratic, in some cases violent or abusive. The behavior may be the result of dementia or alcohol or the side effects of medications. Bills go unpaid. Spending is out of control. The house is falling into disrepair. The family has spoken to Mom, but has gotten nowhere. She refuses to sign a power of attorney or health-care directive, or take any direction or assistance from family. The caller would like to know more about guardianship.

I listen patiently and then start by explaining that guardianship isn't suitable for everyone. And it isn't easy to obtain. Now, that can be a good thing, but it also can be a bad thing. You see, the first step in seeking guardianship is a decision by a court that Mom is incompetent, that she legally cannot make decisions for herself. We have a long history of individual rights in this country. Taking away that freedom is not something Americans take lightly. So, the process of declaring someone incomepetent is not a simple one.

Mom has to be examined by two doctors, who must agree that she is incompetent. (The exact process may vary from state to state.) Then the court appoints an attorney to represent Mom. The attorney must meet with Mom and report back to the court. And here is where the problem usually occurs. If Mom is aware of what is going on, then she may object to the process. She may become angry with her children and tell the attorney assigned to represent her to go back to the judge and tell him she doesn't want to be declared incompetent, that she will fight it.

She tells the attorney that her decisions are hers to make. Her children may think she is incompetent, but where is the line between bad decisions and mental incompetency? It is not an easy one to draw. In many cases, I must tell the children that attempting a guardianship will probably fail. Even worse, it may drive the parent away from seeking or allowing the children to help, actually making the problem worse. In those cases, then, what other options are there?

The problem is that the family (usually the children) is uncomfortable in their role. Roles are reversed. The child assumes a parental role, taking care of the parent, who cannot, or will not, consider the risks that lie ahead.

Yet, the child is waiting for the parent to say yes, and can only go so far on his/her own without that permission. So, nothing is accomplished and the family simply moves from crisis to crisis, always seemingly reacting to events, not preparing for them.

That's when you need to introduce an outside person into the conversation. As I explain to clients, "I can say things to your parents that will be heard differently than if you say them to your parents, or, for that matter, if I say them to my own parents." I may, in fact, say the very same things that the family has been telling Mom. But, now it's different. Mom may have been waiting for the children to take the next step. It isn't just talk anymore. One step turns into the next, and that's how problems get solved. That process can start with an elder law attorney. It can also begin with a trusted advisor, such as your financial planner or accountant.

Another opportunity that so many families let pass is when a crisis occurs. Mom is in the hospital or rehabbing in a subacute care facility. She wants to go home. The family relents. That may, however, be the best time to make a change. It doesn't have to be a permanent one from the start. But, you've got doctors and medical staff to support you as well. If everyone is telling Mom what needs to be done, the focus isn't on the children. It is a whole lot easier for Mom to accept.

Here are a few options to consider. Time isn't on Mom's side. Her health will continue to decline. Sometimes it's a matter of waiting for, and recognizing, the opportunities that present themselves, and then seizing upon them. In the end, Mom may come to accept the changes as necessary, or at least grudgingly allow the children to take the action they know is necessary to insure Mom's continued well-being.

Chapter 9

Medicare

The Big Difference between Medicare and Medicaid

In speaking with people about Medicaid, they will often refer to it as Medicare. Perhaps it's just a slip of the tongue since the two words sound so similar. But, I think, there is very often a fundamental misunderstanding about the two programs. Medicare is the federally funded and state administered health insurance program primarily designed for those individuals over age sixty-five, disabled, or blind. But, here is where the common mistake lies—Medicare does not cover long-term custodial care.

Not that this is different from any employer-sponsored health insurance program. It isn't. What most people don't realize until they need long-term care is that health insurance policies, Medicare included, do not cover custodial nursing home care. Medicare does cover skilled nursing care, but only if you've got an illness or injury from which you can recover. The common illnesses that cause long-term care stays, such as Alzheimers and Parkinsons, have no known cures. Medicare won't help you, which surprises many who are confusing skilled nursing care and custodial care.

In general, if you are enrolled in traditional Medicare, and you've had a hospital stay of at least three days, and then are admitted to a skilled nursing facility, Medicare may pay for a while. If you qualify, Medicare might pay the full cost of the nursing home stay for the first twenty days, and can continue to pay for the next eighty days, but with a deductible of about $135 per day. Some Medicare supplement insurance policies will even pay the cost of that deductible. So, that in the best-case scenario, Medicare may pay up to one hundred days for each "spell of illness."

In order to qualify for this one hundred days of coverage, however, the nursing home resident must be receiving daily "skilled care," and generally must continue to "improve." (Note: Once the Medicare beneficiary has not received a Medicare covered level of care for sixty consecutive days, the beneficiary may again be eligible for the one hundred days of skilled nursing coverage for the next spell of illness).

Although it's never possible to predict at the outset how long Medicare will cover the rehabilitation, from our experience, it usually falls far short of the one-hundred-day maximum. It makes sense, since the recuperative abilities of an eighty-year-old are certainly not what they are for a forty-year-old. But, even if Medicare does cover the one-hundred-day period, what then? What happens after the one hundred days of coverage have been used?

At that point, you're left with paying the bills with your own assets or long-term care insurance, or qualifying for Medicaid, which does cover long-term care, but is a needs-based program. That means you've got to meet certain income and asset limits, but if you were thinking Medicare was going to cover you, then you'll be completely unprepared when it comes to long-term care.

Obamacare—What Do Seniors Need to Know?

Recent studies have shown that most Americans, while fearful of President Obama's new health insurance plan (something that many opposed to the plan have been quick to capitalize on), don't really know what's in it. This is partly due to the President's failure to educate the general public about it. The complexity and broad scope of the law no doubt have something to do with it as well. There are, however, some important features of interest to seniors and their loved ones.

The Affordable Care Act, which Congress passed and the President signed into law in March 2010, will expand health-care coverage for all Americans. No guaranteed benefits under Medicare Part A or Part B are being cut. Some provisions of the new law will take effect immediately. Others will be phased in over the next several years.

Seniors will receive a big benefit immediately, with assistance with the infamous Medicare Part D donut hole. The donut hole is the Part D coverage gap. When a Medicare beneficiary surpasses the prescription drug coverage limit, he or she is then responsible for all prescription drug costs until expenses reach the catastrophic limit. Each year, everyone starts at zero again; so many seniors incur this cost year after year.

A $250 rebate was paid to Medicare beneficiaries who reached the donut hole in 2010 (even by $1). Seniors received these checks automatically. Beginning in 2011, upon reaching the donut hole, seniors will receive a 50% discount on brand-name prescription drugs and a 7% discount on generic prescription drugs. By 2020, the donut hole will be gone, and Medicare beneficiaries will instead pay 25% of the cost until they reach catastrophic coverage levels.

Another change beginning in 2011 will be coverage for preventative care. Medicare will cover one annual wellness exam for each beneficiary. There will be no cost sharing for these services.

Also beginning in 2011, Medicare Advantage plans will have to reduce members' out-of-pocket expenses for some more costly services and for members who use the most health care. The Advantage plans must continue to provide the same benefits available under Medicare Parts A and B. Currently, Advantage plans are paid 14% more than it would cost to cover the same person in traditional Medicare. Over the next several years, the new law will reduce that number to 1%. Plans that receive a high government rating will receive bonus payments, so seniors considering an Advantage plan should look for a plan in existence at least five years, and one that carries a high government rating.

The Community Living Assistance Services and Supports Act (CLASS) establishes a national long-term care insurance program. The program is intended to help pay for some future long-term care services and support.

The new law also provides better information and accountability for nursing home care. It promotes home- and community-based services by providing financial incentives to the states to offer greater assistance for those who choose to remain at home rather than residing in a nursing facility. This signifies recognition by the government that more people want to remain at home (where it is less expensive to administer care). It will be interesting to see if this becomes a trend as 77 million baby boomers start to turn sixty-five.

The new law does include provisions requiring those with higher incomes to pay for Medicare. Beginning in 2011, some will see higher premiums for Part D benefits. Additionally, the Medicare tax rate for households with high income will increase, and the Medicare tax will be applied to unearned income (investment income, royalties, rent, etc.)

The Affordable Care Act is very complicated, and this review covers only a few key elements of importance to seniors. It is clear, however, that while President Obama and Congress have attempted to address some long-term care concerns, the need for planning is as urgent as ever. The government will not come to the rescue. It is up to each one of us to protect ourselves, and a carefully constructed long-term care plan will go a long way to providing that security.

I'm Turning Sixty-Five—Should I Enroll in Medicare?

Much has been written about the oldest baby boomers starting to turn sixty-five in 2011 and what it might mean for the future of long-term care in this country. But from a practical standpoint, there are decisions that each new senior must make that so many are unaware of. Take Medicare for example. More Americans than ever are working beyond what once was the "automatic" retirement age of sixty-five. How does that impact Medicare eligibility?

Most people know that Medicare is the government health insurance program for seniors and the disabled. For many years, turning sixty-five in this country has meant collecting Social Security and enrolling in Medicare. Except that for new seniors now, Social Security won't start until they turn sixty-six years old. Many may then assume that age sixty-six applies to Medicare—it doesn't—or they may simply choose to wait to enroll in Medicare, which could be a big mistake. That's because you could limit your options in the future, and it could cost you more money in premiums for the rest of your life.

Even if you are working and have health insurance benefits through your employer when you turn sixty-five, you should sign up for Medicare Part A, which covers hospitalization expenses. The initial enrollment period is six months, beginning three months before and continuing through three months after your birthday. However, when during that six-month period you sign up also matters. If you sign up before the month of your birthday, then your coverage starts on the first day of the month of your birthday. Sign up during your birthday month, and coverage begins the month after. Sign up later than that, and your beginning date will be even later, possibly three or four months later.

What about Medicare Part B, which covers doctors' bills? When should you sign up for that? It is possible to sign up for Part A but not Part B. Part B carries a separate premium (unlike Part A, which has none) that, when you collect Social Security, is deducted from your Social Security payment. The premium ranges from $96.40 to $110.50 for most people. Because it is optional, some may decide to delay signing up for it if they have other insurance, through their employer or former employer, for example. If you wait, however, you could be hit with higher premiums,

10% more for each year you could have signed up and didn't. And that lasts for the rest of your life.

But, the rules on when you need to sign up are confusing. Most should enroll at age sixty-five or when they retire, whichever is later—maybe. If you still have health insurance through your employer or your spouse's employer, you might be able to delay signing up, as long as there are at least twenty employees in your company. Otherwise, you should enroll. There are also special rules for federal government workers and other groups.

Medicare Part D is the prescription drug coverage introduced a few years ago. Part D rules differ from Parts A and B. Enroll too late, and there is also a premium penalty, 1% for each month you wait. If you have "creditable" drug coverage from your employer's plan, then the penalty may not be imposed. Your employer must tell you each year whether its' plan is better than Medicare's.

Medigap insurance covers what Medicare doesn't. So, for example, it may cover some of your Medicare co-pays. These plans are regulated by the government, meaning there are a few basic plans that will cover certain standard things. The more comprehensive the plan is, the higher the premium. Switching in and out of these plans can be tricky. If you want to change plans without going through a medical screening process, there are separate rules that apply.

Another option that Medicare offers is called Medicare Advantage. Most Advantage plans are HMO-managed care plans. If you are enrolled in one of these plans, you don't get Parts A and B, and you don't need a Medigap policy. The premium will generally be lower, but the negatives to these plans are similar to other HMOs in that your options for treatment may be more limited.

Turning sixty-five is a milestone. Making a decision on Medicare enrollment will have long-term ramifications, so do your research and choose wisely.

Chapter 10

VA Benefits

The Best Kept Secret in Long-Term Care Planning

When it comes to government benefits to cover long-term care, the focus immediately turns to the Medicaid program. However, there is an important, unknown, VA benefit available to wartime veterans and their widowed spouses who are facing substantial medical and care expenses.

Most VA benefits are based on a disability during a veteran's wartime service; however, this non–service-connected pension is available for individuals who are disabled due to issues of old age, such as Alzheimer's, Parkinson's, multiple sclerosis, and other physical disabilities. These benefits can be a blessing for the disabled individual who may not yet need a nursing home, providing as much as nearly $2,000 per month.

A specific portion of the program of particular importance is "Aid and Attendance," and is available to a veteran who is not only disabled, but has the additional requirement of needing the aid and attendance of another person in order to avoid the hazards of his or her daily environment. What that means in plain English is that someone needs to help you prepare meals, bathe, dress, and take care of yourself. The applicant must be determined to be "permanently and totally disabled," meaning he or she is in need of aid and attendance on a regular basis. Someone housebound or in an assisted-living facility and over sixty-five is presumed to be in need of aid and attendance.

There are substantial limitations related to income and assets. It is very confusing to determine what the countable income is that is measured by the VA. Income is determined by taking gross income and subtracting all unreimbursed recurring medical expenses to determine a lower income, which is income for VA purposes and is the number used to determine eligibility.

The asset limit is approximately $40,000 for single individuals, $80,000 for married couples. Unlike Medicaid, there is no penalty for transferring assets out of one's name to qualify for benefits. However, since the applicant may need nursing home care in the future, these same transfers can result in a Medicaid penalty. It is important to consult with an elder law attorney, who can often work out a plan to qualify for VA benefits and at the same time devise a plan to pay for nursing home care, should it be necessary.

Can I Get Medicaid if I Already Get VA Benefits?

I am always explaining how the various sources of payment for long-term care don't mesh well together. That is certainly true when it comes to VA Aid and Attendance and Medicaid benefits. There are quite a few misconceptions. One is the idea that by receiving VA benefits in an assisted-living facility, a resident will later be ineligible for Medicaid assisted-living benefits.

In most instances, that statement is incorrect and leads many veterans to forego as much as $1,949 of tax free income each month that can help pay for assisted-living care. But it is easy to understand why so many make this mistake. It's because the Medicaid waiver programs that pay for this type of care have an income cap of $2,022 per month. So, naturally, the concern is that the additional VA income will push me over that income cap.

Except that not all income is treated as income for Medicaid purposes. The VA Aid and Attendance benefit falls into that category. In most states, it does not constitute "countable income." I should also note that Medicaid won't deny an application if someone does not apply for VA benefits. That can also be a point of confusion since Medicaid does require applicants to apply for other benefits that they may be eligible for, such as disability.

Another point of confusion is that while the VA benefit is not counted for eligibility purposes, it is included with all other income when determining the amount of contribution toward the cost of care. This is the cost sharing aspect to many Medicaid programs. How much you pay for your own care and how much Medicaid pays depends on your income. However, once the VA receives notification of Medicaid benefits received, it will reduce its pension to $90 per month.

As you can see, it's tough navigating through the long-term care system alone. It can cost you literally thousands of dollars a year if you don't get the right information.

How VA Benefits Could Have Saved One Family

Julius was a World War II veteran, who died in 1986. Julia lived independently until 2003 when, at age eighty-three, she moved to an assisted-living facility.

Julia lived in that facility for almost seven years actively participating in events and socializing with other residents. It was at that point, however, that her family moved Julia to a nursing home. They were worried that if she did not have the private funds to pay for her care in a nursing home of their choosing, but applied for Medicaid just before entering a facility, they could not be sure that she would be placed in a suitable nursing home. So, they moved her before she ran out of funds. She is now ninety-one and has not handled the move well. Her health is rapidly deteriorating. She no longer socializes with other residents and rarely speaks, even to family members who visit.

Julia's family was unaware of the VA's Aid and Attendance program, which Julia could have qualified for back in 2003 upon her move to the assisted-living facility. She has lost out on nearly $90,000 in benefits over that seven-year period. That money could have kept Julia in the place where she had thrived, for possibly two more years, before a move had to be made.

Who knows? Maybe her dementia would not have progressed as far if she stayed in the environment in which she had grown accustomed. It's also possible that she may pass away within those two years without ever having to move. Unfortunately, Julia's family didn't know about the VA benefit and they never thought to consult with an elder law attorney. By tapping into any and all possible sources of payment, we can often keep your loved ones in the safest and best environment for them, and reduce the likelihood that you are forced to make a decision purely because you are out of money. Julia's family learned this all too late.

What Happens When a Veteran Dies While a Claim is Pending?

This is a common enough scenario, especially when it seems that the VA is taking longer to process claims than ever before. As with most VA questions, however, the answer is not so simple. It depends on the facts of the particular situation. But first let's review.

Specifically, we are talking about a specific VA program (of which there are many) called Aid and Attendance. This is a non–service-connected pension available to wartime veterans and their spouses who are deemed disabled and in need of aid and attendance. The disability stems not from a service-related injury, but typically from declining health caused by the aging process. Veterans and their surviving spouses can qualify for as much as $1,949 per month of income to help pay the costs of that care.

But, as most applicants are elderly, and the application process can take months, some die while their claims are "pending." VA regulations provide that certain "qualified" persons can continue on with the application. Those persons include the veteran's spouse and the veteran's children. However, not all spouses or all children are "qualified."

The spouse must have been married to the veteran at the time of the veteran's death, lived with the veteran continuously from the date of marriage to the date of death, and not remarried. The child must be under age eighteen or one who became permanently incapable of self-support before reaching eighteen or who is not yet twenty-three and pursuing a course of instruction at an approved educational institution. In each case, that qualified member can complete the VA claim process.

And what if you don't fall into any of the above situations? Then the claim dies with the veteran. However, any person who paid for the veteran/claimant's last illness and burial expenses may file for accrued benefits, to be reimbursed for those out-of-pocket costs. If, for example, the veteran was single and a child was paying for care at home or at an assisted-living facility or nursing home, as long as the expenses can be linked to the last illness, the child can seek reimbursement from the VA. For many families, that can mean recouping as much as $10,000 in VA benefits on an application that may have been pending for six months before the parent died.

144

VA Extended Care Benefits

Understanding the maze of laws and benefits that form our long-term care system is a full-time job. That's why I devoted my practice exclusively to elder and disability planning. A few weeks ago, I was reminded of that fact when I was asked what I know about a particular VA program that provides adult day care services for a small co-pay. This clearly didn't sound like the Aid and Attendance program that in the past several years we have incorporated into our planning arsenal. So, I decided to investigate, and here's what I learned.

The VA doesn't do a good job of publicizing its benefits and services; therefore, getting accurate information is never easy. There is a program of services under what the VA calls the Geriatric and Extended Care Program. These include programs that provide care in a veteran's home or in a community setting, such as adult day care; specialized services for rehabilitation following amputation, stroke, traumatic brain injury, and spinal cord injury; physical therapy; and home hospice care. Keep in mind that the range of services can vary greatly, depending on where you live and which health-care network the VA has charged with providing those services.

Uncovering and understanding the eligibility requirements is the harder part. Unlike the Aid and Attendance program, which is available to veterans and their spouses, the Extended Care Program is only available to veterans who received a discharge under honorable conditions. It is, however, not limited to veterans who served during wartime (again, unlike Aid and Attendance).

There is a co-pay requirement applicable to the non–service-connected pension veteran, that is, a veteran who's injury or illness is not linked to his military service (which is the case with most of our elderly clients). In order to be eligible, the veteran's income must not exceed the maximum annual pension rate for the Aid and Attendance program. The co-pay generally ranges from $5 to $97 per day, depending on the particular service received.

The Extended Care Program is another option, another piece of the long-term care puzzle. And with proper guidance, our clients may be able to tap into a valuable source that will help lessen the risk that they will run out of money, and provide options when they reach the next step in the long-term care journey.

Chapter 11

The Effects of Alzheimer's and Dementia

The Uncertainty of Alzheimer's Disease

So often, when working with families who are struggling to care for a loved one with dementia, the most frustrating part is the uncertainty of the condition from day to day. The recent case in Minnesota of Verne Gagne highlights that very clearly.

Verne Gagne was a prominent professional wrestler with the American Wrestling Association (AWA) in the 1960s and 1970s, and later became a promoter. The AWA eventually lost its big stars, such as Hulk Hogan and Jesse Ventura, to the World Wrestling Federation. Verne is now eighty-two and suffers from Alzheimer's disease, while residing in a nursing home. That is where he had an altercation with a ninety-seven-year-old resident and put a wrestling move on the resident, slamming his body to the ground. The other man broke his hip and died several weeks later. The police are investigating the incident, but there is a consensus of opinion that Mr. Gagne should not be charged with a crime because he didn't know what he was doing. A tragic story, but with similarities that are all too familiar to families who have loved ones with Alzheimer's. It is the uncertain, sometimes violent and erratic, behavior that can be most frustrating and frightening.

Although no one can be sure what caused Verne Gagne to act in the way he did, we know that Alzheimer's patients very often lose their short-term memory but are able to conjure memories of events and people from forty or fifty years ago, or more. Gagne's skill as a wrestler made him more dangerous than the average resident. First, he was more physically fit than the average resident. Second, while he was losing his short-term memory, he was prone to recalling events from his past, such as his days wrestling. Perhaps it is that memory, programmed into his brain, that caused him to perform a wrestling move on his roommate.

It is this type of unpredictability that often turns a family's world upside down. Dad can be living comfortably in a facility one day, and the next he can become extremely agitated and aggressive, causing the facility to ask the family to move him because they can't accommodate his needs, or because of concern for the safety of other residents.

This is just another reason why families cannot wait and react to a loved one's long-term care needs. Whenever possible, preventative measures need to be taken. So often, we see families plan as if Mom's or Dad's current condition, while tragic and upsetting, will remain static and unchanging. That is usually not the case, and misjudging the situation can be worse than anyone imagined.

Who knows what could have been done to prevent Verne Gagne from acting out? After all, this was not the first altercation between Gagne and his roommate. The lesson to be learned on a broader level, however, is to recognize the unpredictability of Alzheimer's, and dementia in general. Take action before, not after, it becomes necessary. I am sure everyone involved in Verne Gagne's case is reexamining what they could have done differently.

One of the Clearest Warning Signs of Dementia

More often than not, the first call we receive about a prospective client who is facing long-term care concerns comes from a child or other family member, rather than the senior client. And so often the caller expresses surprise at recently discovering that Mom or Dad is slipping. It is how that discovery is made, which shows us there are telltale signs of dementia and Alzheimer's that families should look for. And new research backs up my anecdotal evidence.

Experts on Alzheimer's disease note that one of the first signs of dementia is confusion surrounding money and credit. This confusion can result in not paying bills on time. It may also lead to being the victim of a senior scam. Sometimes it is a "friend" helping the senior write checks to the "friend" or multiple checks to various charities to which the senior never previously expressed any interest.

Issues surrounding money and finances are complicated. Many families never talk about money. It's a taboo subject. Likewise, the issue of competency is complex. It is not a bright-line determination. As I often explain, whether I have a broken leg or not can be determined with certainty. An X-ray will usually settle the issue. The brain is a more tricky issue. Just because you have a diagnosis of dementia does not automatically mean you are incompetent. The mental decline is gradual, with many ups and downs. But over time, it is a downward decline. That's what makes it so difficult to know when someone can no longer handle their own affairs.

Waiting too long, however, has some very real dangers. Take the case of Dr. Max Gomez. His case was highlighted in a recent *New York Times* article. You may know of his son, Dr. Max Gomez, for many years the medical correspondent for CBS News. Max, the son, lives in New York. Dad was living alone in Miami, and over time began experiencing problems dealing with his finances. By the time his son learned of the problems, Dad had lost everything, including his condominium to foreclosure.

Unfortunately, Dr. Gomez's case is all too common. The lesson to be learned is to have conversations about finances with your loved one early on. If possible, establish a system by which you'll get notice if Mom or

Dad skips paying bills. Taking a look at the checkbook for money going in and out is also a good idea. It may be an uncomfortable subject, but the pain of losing everything is far greater.

Early-Onset Alzheimer's

Claire is in her late forties and divorced. She owns her own home worth approximately $250,000, but with a substantial mortgage with a balance of $150,000, which probably describes a lot of people. Except that Claire has Alzheimer's. Although the disease mostly affects the elderly, early-onset Alzheimer's is not uncommon. It is hereditary and can even hit people in their thirties.

I received a call from Jane, her daughter. Claire can't work, and has no income. The home is a mess and falling into disrepair because she can no longer take care of it. Claire is temporarily living with her father, who is in his late seventies. He pays the mortgage, taxes, and upkeep on her home, although he is getting on in years and his health is failing. The family has no direction and is just living day by day with no idea when the nightmare will end.

Jane asked if we could help save the home. Could the home be transferred out of Claire's name? My answer, unfortunately, was no.

"How long ago was your mom diagnosed," I asked.

Jane told me it was about three years ago. Claire refused to consider moving, and Jane and her grandfather have been supporting Claire until now, but they have reached a point where that is no longer possible.

So, the home is on the market. But after closing costs and paying off the mortgage, there isn't much left. Jane was also hoping to recoup for herself and her grandfather the money they spent supporting Claire. Most importantly, there is the matter of providing care for Claire, hopefully in an assisted-living facility, at a cost of $4,500 per month. When her condition worsens, the next step is a nursing home, and that costs $10,000 per month.

I sympathized with Jane, but didn't have any magic solution. She simply waited too long before making what, no doubt, are tough decisions. So what should she have done?

Three years ago when the diagnosis was made is when the family needed to act. Selling the home and/or moving assets into a trust and out of Claire's name would have made sense. Because there is a five-year look back for Medicaid benefits, the family would need to manage Claire's care and costs during that time period. But managed correctly, they could have had assets left after five years, in trust, that could be used together with available government benefits to get the best care possible for Claire. They would have had options.

Now, they are selling a home falling into disrepair, in a down market. Not the best scenario for Claire, who needs as much money as she can squeeze out of the sale to provide for her future care. This is a lesson for all of us. If we delay making tough decisions, they only get tougher.

I felt the despair in Jane's voice, "How can our country let this happen?" she asked.

I didn't have an answer for that one either.

Alzheimer's Disease
and Government Shutdowns

A new survey by the MetLife Foundation indicates that more Americans fear Alzheimer's disease than any other disease except cancer—and in a few years that just might change. Approximately 1,000 Americans were interviewed last fall. Thirty-one percent indicated they most feared Alzheimer's disease, ahead of heart disease, stroke, and diabetes. Forty-one percent said they most feared cancer. Interestingly, four years earlier, 38% said they feared cancer most versus 20% for Alzheimer's. With baby boomers entering retirement, presumably, the gap will continue to close. The survey also confirmed some other suspicions.

Nearly one in four interviewed said they were concerned about needing to provide long-term care for a loved one with Alzheimer's. Less than one in five said they had made any plans for the possibility of getting Alzheimer's. Only two in five people said they have had discussions with their families about Alzheimer's. Four in five adults admitted that they have made no financial arrangements for the cost of care should they develop the disease. And here's one final statistic—63% of those surveyed acknowledged they know little or nothing about Alzheimer's disease.

One thing is clear. Although the average American is concerned, he or she is not doing anything about it. The problem isn't going away, however, and will only continue to intensify. The government isn't going to help either, if recent developments are any indication. Last spring Congress and the president only avoided a government shutdown at the eleventh hour when they reached tentative agreement on federal budget cuts. The message is clear. You've got to look out for yourself and your family. Others won't do it for you.

Chapter 12

The Home

Saving the Home

Sarah was a good daughter. For as long as she could remember, she'd been in the role of caretaker. When she was little, and Mom was hospitalized for three and a half weeks, Sarah had taken over running the family—even though she was only thirteen. And that wasn't the only time.

But it seemed like Sarah had finally escaped that role—until three years ago, when Mom had a stroke. Since Mom could no longer care for herself, Sarah moved back home and took over Mom's care. And she's been doing it for the past three years, but now it's gotten to the point where Mom needs more care then Sarah can give.

Mom owns a $350,000 house, and she'd like to give the house to Sarah as a way of saying thank you for all that Sarah has done for her. But when Mom and Sarah checked around, they were told that if Mom gifts the house to Sarah, she will be ineligible for Medicaid for years, and it may even be a criminal act!

Sarah came to us very upset. I calmly told her that there's a way for Mom to transfer the house to Sarah and preserve Mom's eligibility for Medicaid. The law states that you can give a home to an adult child who resided in the home for at least two years, if the child provided care, which permitted Mom to stay at home, rather than in an institution or facility.

In other words, if a child moves back home and cares for a parent, and if that child's care has kept the parent out of a nursing home for at least the last two years, then the home may be given to the child without Medicaid penalties.

So, how should Sarah document her care for Mom? The best thing would be to keep a log or journal that sets forth specific incidents or events that, but for the child's care, might have resulted in Mom's institutionalization. For instance, note things like gas burners not being shut off, water left running in the tub, Mom's wandering, or other medically dangerous actions.

In addition, it would be helpful to have statements from other family members or neighbors telling of any events or circumstances that reinforce Sarah's position. Finally, it would be most helpful to have a letter from a physician and/or visiting nurse or home health-care provider saying that Sarah's care did in fact keep Mom out of the nursing home for at least two years. Ideally, you want Mom's condition to be documented before the two-year period starts.

I explained this to Sarah and her Mom, and they were both delighted that all of Sarah's good deeds will not go unrewarded. Mom can give the house to Sarah and still qualify for Medicaid.

FYI: There are other situations where the home may be transferred without penalty. They include transfers to the following:

- The spouse

- A minor, blind, or disabled child

- A sibling who has an equity interest in the home and who has resided there for at least one year before the Medicaid applicant became institutionalized.

Reverse Mortgages

Much has been written about the reverse mortgage. A reverse mortgage differs from a traditional mortgage in that the borrower/homeowner does not make any regular payments to the lender to repay the loan. The loan is repaid either upon the sale of the property or when the homeowner dies. The borrower must be sixty-two years or older to be eligible, and the fees associated with these loans are generally higher than for a traditional mortgage since the lender will not know exactly when the loan will be repaid. The payouts come in many forms, i.e., a lump sum, regular monthly payments, or a line of credit that can be tapped at any time and in any amount up to the limits.

As an elder law attorney, I am often asked my opinion about reverse mortgages. I think in the right situation they can be beneficial. When a senior homeowner wants additional income, and has other assets he/she doesn't want to sell, liquidate, or otherwise use, but is sitting on a substantial home equity, then it can be a great option.

However, so often I see people who can't afford to remain at home. They are on a fixed income. Taxes, insurance, and general costs of living are rising, and they need additional funds to sustain their standard of living. If they just had a little extra every month to meet their monthly bills, everything would be OK. Except that they haven't accounted for long-term care needs.

So, they take a reverse mortgage. For a while, perhaps, they can meet their monthly bills. But then the long-term care costs begin. Pretty soon those costs are running into several thousand dollars a month or more and start eating into the mortgage limit. The senior starts to cut back on other expenses, typically the maintenance on the home. The home starts to fall into disrepair, thereby reducing the value of the one major asset the senior has left. When the reverse mortgage is completely tapped out, the senior can't afford to pay for his/her care.

Now, he needs to go to a nursing home but has no money to pay for it, and must sell the house. It doesn't help that the house may need a lot of work, certainly not in a down real estate market as we have seen in the last few years in many areas of the country.

In these cases, the reverse mortgage is not the best fit because it lulls people into a false sense that they can stay in their home. It helps them avoid addressing the awful question of what happens if I outlive my money and I need long-term care? It is not an easy decision to sell the home you've lived in for most of your adult life. But isn't it better to downsize, reduce your expenses, and still live independently than to hang on in a home you can no longer afford and then run out of money at the exact time when you need it most?

A Closer Look at Reverse Mortgages

Mom and Dad are living in their home, but their health is failing. They do not yet need nursing home–level care, but do need some assistance on a daily basis. Their children are running back and forth, helping to provide care, but it is just too difficult to do on a long-term basis. The plan is to move them to an assisted-living facility. The problem, however, is that they have limited funds to pay for that care. While they intend to sell the home, that won't happen overnight.

An option that has worked well in the past is to take a home equity line of credit and use that line to pay the monthly assisted-living fee (and real estate taxes, insurance, and maintenance) until the home is sold. Except, in today's economy, with the financial industry itself being bailed out, banks are no longer approving these loans, concerned about the credit worthiness of borrowers and the risk of default. So what now?

It may be time to look at a reverse mortgage. Increasingly, this is the only option for seniors. The concern about defaulting loans is not an issue because, by its terms, a reverse mortgage won't be repaid until the borrower dies or sells the home. The ability of the borrower to repay isn't a factor because he/she makes no monthly payments. Hence the term "reverse."

Over the years, I have seen many cases where reverse mortgages have enabled seniors to stay in homes they really couldn't afford any longer and probably should have sold. If they outlive the funds borrowed, typically they are in poor health and now have exhausted their assets completely. It is also true that these loans carry higher transactional fees than traditional mortgages.

However, here, the plan is to sell the home as soon as possible to pay for the next level of care, not hang on too long. And, if a traditional mortgage isn't an option any longer, the higher fees become acceptable given the alternative of the children taking money from their own savings to pay the cost of Mom and Dad's care. With an economy in recession and unemployment rates at their highest in a generation, many children don't have the funds to pay for their parents' long-term care.

That's why, for many, it may be time to take a closer look at the reverse mortgage.

Chapter 13

The Nightmare Stories

How to Lose Medicaid

We get numerous calls each week from people asking for help with a long-term care crisis. One call in particular highlights the dangers for nursing home and resident alike in going it alone when seeking Medicaid.

Alice called us because she had been sued for $80,000 by the nursing home caring for her mother, Florence. Florence had entered the nursing home on private pay, and after spending down her assets qualified for Medicaid. Under Medicaid rules, Florence's Social Security check went to the nursing home and Medicaid paid the rest of the bill. Alice and the nursing home arranged for the check to go directly to the nursing home, and everything was fine for eight years or so.

Alice then moved out of state. Apparently, Social Security assumed that Florence moved too and started sending Florence's checks to her bank account. Alice did not notice this for several months, at least, and neither did the nursing home. After eight years, Florence lost her Medicaid eligibility.

How could this happen? While Alice does not yet have all the facts (she'll find out more as the lawsuit winds through the court system), here's what probably occurred. Because Florence's income was accumulating in her account, once the balance exceeded $2,000, she lost Medicaid eligibility. Florence's Social Security is treated as income in the month received, but if still in her possession the next month, then it is treated as an asset. And each month her balance remained over $2,000, she was Medicaid ineligible—and those lost months can never be recovered. So, every month Florence was running up a bill at the nursing home's private-pay rate.

It is not clear why the nursing home didn't notice the change, or why it took them several months to write to Alice. They did send her a new Medicaid application to complete and file, but she either didn't receive it or didn't act on it. It appears that nobody on either side was following up on it, so Medicaid was never reinstated for the last year of Florence's life. Now, the nursing home is looking to recoup a year's worth of lost payments, and Alice is trying to avoid a judgment that she can't afford to pay.

The sad thing is that this all could have been avoided. Medicaid rules are quite complex. The resident's family and the nursing home needed to keep in contact and stay on top of any changes that could affect Medicaid eligibility. It is easy to miss something that can result in ineligibility, and each month of ineligibility cannot be reversed.

In other words, if you are ineligible this month, you need to fix whatever is causing that so you can become Medicaid eligible next month, but you can't do anything to change this month. That is lost forever.

What is also important to recognize is that once you are approved for Medicaid, you must be careful not to lose that eligibility. What you might think is the most insignificant change can cause a chain of events that will lead to losing benefits. You can't just go on autopilot. That's when things fall through the cracks.

That is exactly what happened here. And now both sides are pointing fingers at each other. Had Alice retained an elder law attorney to file the Medicaid application, both the resident and nursing home would have benefited and, perhaps, this unfortunate result could have been avoided.

Elder Care Point: It is easy to miss something that can result in ineligibility, and each month of ineligibility cannot be reversed.

Is a Child Responsible for
Not Pursuing Medicaid for a Parent?

A recent case in Connecticut highlights how the new Medicaid laws passed as part of the Deficit Reduction Act of 2005 are really hurting nursing homes and families. In that case, the nursing home resident's son signed the admission agreement on behalf of his mother. As in most nursing home agreements, the son was asked to sign as responsible party, which he did not do. Nevertheless, the nursing home advised him verbally that he was the responsible party.

The son then applied for Medicaid benefits on behalf of his mother. He did not, however, follow through on the application process in a timely manner. He failed to provide all the information and documentation that the state needed and did not spend down Mom's assets quickly enough, delaying the application's approval. As a result, months of benefits were lost, never to be regained. These were benefits that the nursing home would have received.

The nursing home sued the son claiming that he undertook an obligation on his mother's behalf, when he signed the admission agreement, to promptly pursue Medicaid benefits. The son, in response, argued that he never signed the agreement, so there was no binding obligation on his part. The court sided with the nursing home, finding that an oral contract was created between the two parties and that the son violated it by not conscientiously following through.

This was a good result for the nursing home, right? Well, not really, when you account for the time and money it took the nursing home to get the judgment. It then has to collect on that judgment, assuming the son doesn't appeal the decision, which will cause the matter to drag on even further. A better result would have been for the nursing home to encourage the son to retain an elder law attorney to represent his mother in the Medicaid application process. Sure, there is an expense involved in hiring someone, but in the end the nursing home would have received Medicaid benefits when it should have, and both sides would have spent a lot less in attorney's fees. It would have been a win-win for both sides.

Transfer of Home
Leads to Medicaid Mess

Here's another situation that illustrates so clearly the dangers of going it alone or getting bad advice when dealing with the common issues and dilemmas that seniors and their families so frequently face. I received a call last week from George in Mississippi. Mom and Dad, living in New Jersey, were no longer able to live alone. They transferred their home to their son and moved in with him in Mississippi. That's when the plan fell apart.

Dad's health deteriorated more rapidly than anticipated, and he needed nursing home care. The couple then spent down their remaining assets and applied for nursing home care for Dad. Meanwhile George placed the New Jersey home up for sale.

Much to their surprise, the family was informed that the state Medicaid office denied Dad's application. Why? Because the transfer of the home to George caused a Medicaid ineligibility period. Dad could not receive Medicaid for four and a half years. They were told that George must give the money back to Mom and Dad, and they must spend it down before Dad will receive Medicaid.

George said that he was prepared to pay for Dad's care, if that was necessary. I told him he would probably need to transfer back the money from the sale to reduce the transfer penalty, but that his parents would not necessarily have to spend down the assets. I advised him, however, to seek the advice of an elder law attorney in Mississippi familiar with the Medicaid laws there before he does anything. It may make more sense for Mom to take some of the money and buy a new home, which would be exempt for Medicaid purposes. There are other strategies that may be beneficial as well and should be explored in greater detail.

The lesson to be learned here is to consult with a professional before making any decisions. There is a maze of laws and services in this country that affect seniors. It is easy to get tripped up by them, and the cost to your family could be enormous.

Assisted-Living Resident with No Money and No Medicaid

Dad has been living in an assisted-living facility for three years at a cost of $4,500 per month. He likes it there, where he is safe and well cared for. There is one small problem. He is running out of money, and the family is becoming desperate.

Fortunately, some states have Medicaid programs that cover assisted-living care, but the rules can vary significantly from nursing home Medicaid. In New Jersey, for example, if income exceeds the Medicaid limit ($2,022 per month in 2011), the assisted-living program won't be an option. For those needing nursing home care, on the other hand, that limit may be higher.

The application process for Medicaid can take several months or longer. If, for example, Dad becomes eligible and applies for Medicaid beginning in February, it might take until April, or longer in some cases, for him to receive approval. In the case of nursing home Medicaid, whenever Dad is approved, Medicaid will pay on his behalf, retroactive to when he first applied (assuming, of course, that he was eligible in that month). Not so for assisted-living Medicaid. Approval is not retroactive.

As elder law attorneys, our focus with clients is on the financial requirements of Medicaid. We always, however, remind clients that we can't forget about the medical requirement. The applicant must require nursing home–level care as determined by a Medicaid nurse who visits the applicant. In some states, this is true even in the case of assisted living. It bears repeating. The assisted-living Medicaid applicant must be certified as needing nursing home–level care. Fail that test, and the asset and income levels are irrelevant.

So, if Dad can't get Medicaid, what then? If he can't pay the bill, he generally won't be able to stay in the assisted-living facility unless the family pays for his care. This is not a great result, but one the family could have avoided. Before he entered the facility, a plan should have been put in place to cover the possibility that he could run out of money. In some cases, that may involve moving assets to a trust or determining what public benefits he can or cannot receive and when (such as VA Aid and Attendance benefits). It may mean choosing a different, less expensive, facility or living arrangement. It all depends on one's particular situation.

The mistake that Dad and his family made was not looking far enough down the road and failing to sit down with someone knowledgeable about the various issues and pitfalls, such as an elder law attorney. The lesson to be learned from this is that you can't wait until the money runs out to answer the question, "What do I do now?"

> **Elder Care Point:** *The assisted-living Medicaid applicant must be certified as needing nursing home–level care. Fail that test, and the asset and income levels are irrelevant.*

Declining Stock Market Leads to Long-Term Care Nightmare

As the current economic crisis deepens, it is becoming increasingly clear that we are heading into uncharted waters, in so many respects. Specifically, however, I am talking about the long-term care arena, and a recent phone call I received highlights this so clearly.

John called concerning his father. Dad owns his home. Home health aides come into the home to assist Dad, but as his health deteriorates and he needs increased care, John believes that Dad will very soon need to move to a nursing facility. Now, here is where it gets interesting.

Dad took a reverse mortgage for $300,000 in a lump sum. John's plan was to invest the money in the market and get a decent rate of return that would help meet Dad's expenses. Well, what happened the following year was that the stock market declined drastically and Dad's investment headed south, too. He lost roughly half of his account value. That was bad enough, but here is the bigger problem. John transferred the money to an account in his name. Not because he intended to keep it, but because it was just easier to manage the funds that way.

When he did that, however, he caused a Medicaid transfer penalty of approximately three and a half years. So what happens when Dad sells his home and uses the sale proceeds (less the amount he pays back to the bank) for his nursing home care? He will be ineligible for Medicaid unless John transfers back the money. The problem is that John no longer has all of it.

I know. You're thinking, "Will Medicaid really deny Dad's application if John can show that the loss in value occurred in the market, and that he didn't take the money?" I don't know. Maybe—maybe not. You see, we are living in unusual times. Many states are struggling with budget deficits. Medicaid is one of the biggest, if not the biggest, program for most states. If the states don't have the money to fund these programs, applying the Medicaid rules as written and imposing a penalty is a real possibility. If Dad is ineligible for three and a half years, then he may never live to receive Medicaid, something the government no doubt may consider.

And this is another example of why you can't afford to be unprepared when it comes to long-term care.

"It's Dad's Money—He Can Do What He Wants with It, Right?"

In February 2006, Congress passed some significant changes to the Medicaid laws that created very dangerous traps for unprepared families needing long-term care. At the time, I wrote about a case in which Granddad gifted his money to Granddaughter, who moved in to care for him. When she could no longer provide the care and applied for Medicaid, she was told, mistakenly, that he was not eligible because of the gifts. It turned out that the Medicaid ineligibility period had expired. We filed for Medicaid on her behalf, and the application was approved. This was a happy ending, but it's one that would not end so happily under the new law.

Recently, I received a call with an all-too-common story. Mom had recently died. Dad moved in with his daughter, Robin, and the plan was for him to live there the rest of his life. At the same time, Dad gifted $150,000 to Robin and her brother, Joe.

"It's Dad's money. He can do what he wants with it," she told me.

Well, I think you can guess what happened. Robin was unprepared for the reality of long-term care. I could hear the stress in her voice as she described the deterioration of Dad's mental and physical state, from the mood swings and erratic behavior to the declining personal hygiene and the inability to walk without assistance. His care needs were increasing, and Robin was unable to handle the increased demands on her time while caring for her own young children.

"I just never expected this," she exclaimed. "I can't do this anymore. I need to get Dad into a nursing home, and he has $50,000 left. What do I do?" she pleaded.

I explained to her that once his money was spent down, he could qualify for Medicaid, but she and Joe would need to return the $150,000. But here was the problem. Robin and Joe had already spent the money, and therefore couldn't return it.

"Well," I told her, "when Dad's remaining $50,000 is spent down, he still won't be Medicaid eligible for another four years. That's because the Medicaid penalty doesn't start until he has less than $2,000 to his name, needs nursing home care, and applies for Medicaid.

"It's so unfair," she cried. "The government is forcing me into poverty to pay for Dad's care."

I patiently explained to her that she and her brother did receive a substantial sum from Dad, money that should be spent for his own care before public funds could be tapped. The sad truth, however, is that, had the family consulted with an elder law attorney before the gifts were made, Dad could have transferred some assets while preserving enough to cover the possibility that he would need long-term care before Medicaid eligibility. Unfortunately, in Robin's case, I didn't have any solution to her problem. She would have to figure out how to care for her Dad or pay out of her own pocket until the Medicaid ineligibility period expired. Sadly, it didn't have to turn out this way. Let it be a cautionary tale for all.

Dad Owns His Home
and Needs Care

A common scenario that I am seeing with increasing frequency is the following fact pattern. Dad owns a home but not much else. He needs nursing home care, but can't get a mortgage to tap into the equity to pay for the care. The home is listed for sale, but in today's market, homes aren't moving quickly. So, the children pay the nursing home bill and the cost to maintain the home, with the expectation that when they sell the home they will repay themselves. The family doesn't have any written documentation to reflect this arrangement, and that's where the problem starts.

So, the children pay for Dad's care and expenses. Maybe they pay by credit card, sometimes by check. Some expenses, such as lawn care, they pay cash. Oftentimes they don't keep records to back up the expenses, and if more than one child is helping out, no one is keeping a running tally of who is paying what.

"We'll figure it all out later," they say.

Finally, the house is sold. Dad gets $200,000 from the sale. The kids estimate that they have spent $150,000 on Dad's behalf and take that amount to repay themselves. Dad then spends down the rest for his care.

Now, it's time to file a Medicaid application. As part of the application, Dad must produce financial records for each account he had in existence, going back five years. The state will examine the home sale and discover the transfer from Dad to the children. It will treat the transfer as subject to a Medicaid penalty, unless the children can prove the money was repayment for goods or services that Dad received. And that proof must be by documentary evidence. Dad won't be eligible for benefits for a year or more, depending on the state he lives in.

"Bring the money back and spend it down," the state will say.

So what can this family do? There are a few options. Some involve applying for Medicaid immediately. Others involve family members paying for Dad's care, and then getting reimbursed later. However, the one common element to each option is that there is a written agreement in the form of a note and a mortgage on Dad's home to secure the loan. The paper trail is the key. Without it, the children will never be able to prove that the transfer was for value, and won't be able to recoup the money, in some cases hundreds of thousands of dollars, advanced for their parent's care.

What the children should do is seek proper advice and guidance—and the sooner the better. You don't want to wait until filing the application to find all this out because, of course, by then it is too late. You'll have a Medicaid penalty, and probably no way to pay for it.

The Right Way and the Wrong Way to Hire a Home Health Aide

As long-term care needs increase and families want to keep their loved ones at home, hiring home health aides often becomes necessary. Paying an aide, however, if not done correctly, can cause Medicaid ineligibility years later, after funds run out. Consider the following very common scenario.

Cathy hires a home health aide at $700 per week cash, or $3,000 per month. She keeps the aide three years until her funds run out, and now needs round-the-clock care. A nursing home becomes the only option.

She applies for Medicaid but is told, "Sorry, you're not eligible for fifteen months. You'll have to private pay until then."

Of course, Cathy has no more money. She'll have to come up with the funds some other way, perhaps from family members. But at $10,000 per month or more, that may not be possible. How did Cathy get into this mess? Because Medicaid treated her payments to the aide ($108,000) as transfers subject to a penalty.

Qualifying for Medicaid requires spending down assets to less than $2,000. Transferring assets may cause Medicaid ineligibility if you do not receive something of equal value back. Medicaid calls this a "penalty." However, and this is key, you must prove to Medicaid that assets transferred are not subject to a penalty.

If you pay the aide cash (or by check) and don't keep proper records, Medicaid will assess a penalty. The penalty is calculated by dividing the transferred amount by the average cost of nursing home care. When one applies for Medicaid, there is now a five-year look back period, meaning Medicaid will look back five years from the date of the application to find these transfers. They will add together all the transfers made during that time. The penalty will begin when all other assets have been spent down and the individual enters a nursing home and applies for Medicaid.

Of course, that is exactly the time when you have no more money. The state presumes you gifted the money, and so will tell you to get it back, use it, and then, after it's gone, to come back and they will pay for your care. But you didn't gift the money, so you can't get it back.

How can you avoid Cathy's problem? By keeping records to prove the payments were not gifts, and by avoiding using cash, which is difficult to trace. It is also a good idea to generate detailed invoices of the services that you purchased. Another, perhaps better, solution is to hire a home health agency that will supply the aide. It will cost more than hiring an aide directly, but your contract with the agency will insure that Medicaid can never challenge the payments as gifts. And in the long run it may cost you less because you won't be stuck with a Medicaid penalty.

> ***Elder Care Point:*** *Transferring assets may cause Medicaid ineligibility if you do not receive something of equal value back. Medicaid calls this a "penalty."*

Dangers of an Unlicensed Home Health Aide

For many families, keeping their elderly loved one at home will require in-home assistance. There are many quality home health-care companies in the area, so finding one isn't a problem. But I find so often that clients don't go through a licensed agency because of the cost. Although I have written in the past about the Medicaid problem of hiring aides directly and paying cash, there is another very real risk—safety. The following story is one, unfortunately, I have heard more than once.

Dorothy found an aide to care for Dad through an agency she had learned of from a friend. I know many of the quality licensed agencies in the area, but had never heard of this one. Dorothy paid a fee to the agency, who sent an aide to her dad's home, but her financial dealings with the agency ended there. She paid the aide directly in cash. I cautioned Dorothy that she didn't really know anything about the agency or the person they were sending, but she said she interviewed the woman, who seemed pleasant enough. And Dorothy was in a bind because Dad had run out of money, so she was paying out of her own pocket. The aide she had found herself and who had stayed with Dad for three years was going back to her native country, so Dorothy needed to find someone quickly.

What happened after one month was Dorothy's worst nightmare. On one of her daily visits to Dad's home, she found him bruised and battered, in a semiconscious state. He had been beaten by the aide, who claimed not to know what happened. Dorothy called the police. They immediately arrested the aide, and Dad was transported to the hospital.

Upon further investigation, Dorothy discovered that the agency was neither licensed nor insured. The owner disappeared, probably to reappear under another agency name. And unfortunately Dad's injuries were of a severity that he could no longer stay at home, but needed nursing home care. Dorothy felt terrible, but her predicament is hardly uncommon. When trying to make ends meet, safety was compromised. Bringing a complete stranger into a home to care for a defenseless senior should not be taken lightly. Background checks must be done. Training is important. There is a reason going through a reputable agency is more expensive.

However, if a long-term care plan had been put in place, well before Dad needed care, perhaps Dorothy would not have been strapped for cash.

Dad would have had the money to pay for his own care, and maybe government benefits could have been tapped to help out. Dorothy would then have hired the licensed agency, safety precautions would have been taken, and a tragedy could have been avoided.

Why Long-Term Care is a Woman's Worst Nightmare

I could hear the panic in Patty's voice. Her husband, Phil's health had been steadily declining for years, and Patty had been his primary caregiver. But last week he fell at home, breaking his hip, and now he's in a subacute facility. The recovery process hasn't gone well, in part because of Phil's age and partly because of the toll that Alzheimer's has taken on his mind. Patty is now facing the prospect of either long-term care at a cost of $11,000 per month or, in an effort to keep the cost down, trying to bring him home and provide much of the care herself, supplementing it with a few hours of home aide assistance.

"Phil never wanted to talk about long-term care, and so we never did plan for this," she tells me. It's a classic scenario, and one that so often is more damaging to the wife than the husband. How so?

Patty's situation is a typical one. At seventy-two, she's six years younger than Phil. Add the fact that women have a longer life expectancy than men, and chances are that the husband will need long-term care first. And if the couple hasn't planned for it, they'll likely spend most of their savings on his care. Patty and Phil have $400,000 of assets plus their house. Without any guidance, Patty could be left with as little as $110,000 and the house before the state will help pay for Phil's care.

What about their income? Patty will lose much of that too, toward Phil's care. He has Social Security of $1,500 and a pension of $2,500, while she has only Social Security of $500 because Patty spent many years tending to the needs of her family. She'll get to keep approximately $1,500 of Phil's income when he qualifies for Medicaid, not enough to meet her expenses. Then, when he dies, she'll take another hit because Phil chose the maximum pension for his life. There is no survivor option for Patty. Add to that the fact that she will only receive one Social Security check (Phil's, because it is the larger of the two), and her income will drop to $1,500. It is therefore so important for Patty to protect as much of their assets as she can to replace the income she will lose.

And when Patty needs care, it will likely be more expensive and difficult to administer. Why? Because she won't have a healthy spouse living with her to care for her at home. Chances are she'll need to hire more care, and she'll be more likely to need nursing home care earlier. Her children will need to take on a greater role in order to fill the void.

One more thing—Patty's concern about keeping costs down is causing her to take on more of the caregiver role herself. That can take a physical and emotional toll, and may contribute to a more rapid decline in her health. Had the couple planned for this possibility well in advance, tapping into available sources of payment, such as long-term care insurance or government benefits, Patty would be more inclined to pay for additional help.

When you consider all these factors together, it becomes clear that, for many couples, it is the woman who is at greater risk. Patty now realizes it too. Fortunately, she isn't too late in reaching out to us. We can still help her protect something. Granted, it would have been better had she called sooner, but it's better late than never.

How $250,000 Went up in Smoke

Karen's husband, Scott, passed away several years ago, but she continued to live in the home where they had raised their family. Karen was now struggling with the effects of dementia. But she wouldn't hear of it when her children talked about moving her to a safer environment. So they arranged for a home aide to provide some assistance. However, Karen had no other assets from which to pay for care, so her children chipped in. Nevertheless, Karen was home alone for long periods of time. And that's when tragedy struck.

Karen was using the stove, and although no one is really sure how it happened, a fire started in the kitchen, which destroyed the entire home. Miraculously, Karen escaped serious injury. Her family considered themselves lucky. They now knew, almost too late, that Karen needed more supervision. They planned to take the homeowners insurance money and use it to place her in an assisted-living facility. That's when Karen's family got a second shock.

You see, Karen had never increased the insurance limits on her home. As its value increased, along with the costs of material and labor to rebuild, her policy limits remained unchanged. So, all she received from the insurance company was $100,000, even though the fair market value of the now-destroyed home was over $500,000.

When Karen sells the now-vacant lot, she'll get a bit more cash to help pay her long-term care needs, but it won't be anywhere near $500,000. The end result is that Karen lost at least a quarter of a million dollars in that fire, along with the rest of her belongings. There is now a greater chance that she'll run out of money. So, while Karen and her family were lucky that she escaped the fire with her health intact, she wasn't so lucky when it came to her finances. She now is much worse off than her family could have ever imagined.

There are a couple of lessons to be learned here. First, make sure you check your insurance coverage and keep it up to date. But, the broader lesson to be taken from this tragedy is that a failure to act can have catastrophic consequences—far worse than the decisions you are trying to avoid making. As the saying goes, "A failure to plan is a plan for failure."

The Second-Marriage Long-Term Care Problem

Recently, I have seen an increasing number of second marriage "horror stories." A call we received last week again highlights the danger. Mel, a seventy-year-old widower, moved into a continuing care retirement community. He met Wendy, a seventy-five-year-old widow, and developed a fast friendship. Eventually it led to marriage. Mel and Wendy promised to care for each other "until death do they part." That's when the problems began for Mel.

A few years after their wedding, Wendy began a physical and mental decline that led to her need for assisted-living and then nursing home care. Wendy had savings of $200,000, as did Mel, but no long-term care insurance. She lived long enough to spend her entire savings plus much of Mel's. When she died, Mel had only $75,000 in savings left. Mel and Wendy were completely unprepared for how long-term care would affect them. And Mel was totally unaware that Wendy could have qualified for Medicaid before she died.

Now, Mel's health is declining. He never before shared his finances with his children, so they were shocked to learn that his savings had been depleted. They are concerned that he will not be able to stay in the retirement community when his remaining funds are exhausted. I asked Mel, Jr. what his Dad's agreement with the community says about that. He doesn't know because he's never seen the contract. Dad said he could handle things himself, signing the forty-plus–page contract without getting a second opinion. Well, he clearly can't take care of things any longer. Mel, Jr. and his siblings will now have to make some tough decisions. But instead of having a plan in place with options to choose from, the family instead is reacting in crisis mode. This is not the best situation to be in and one that could have easily been avoided by planning ahead.

Laura's Dilemma—Don't Let It Be Yours

Laura called me in desperation. Her husband, Rick, had recently been hospitalized with heart problems. He is also struggling with the onset of Alzheimer's disease. Laura has been able to administer care to this point, but it has taken its toll on her physically and mentally, and her children are concerned about her health. Laura made a commitment to keep Rick at home. With the encouragement of her kids, she called to inquire about benefits available to help pay for in home care, which she expects to be nearly round the clock.

Rick and Laura's combined income is about $2500 per month from Social Security and a pension. While they own their own home worth about $400,000, their savings are down to $50,000. There is no way Laura can afford the cost of Rick's care and maintaining the home, and still have something left to support herself. They have no long-term care insurance policies. Laura figured there must be a government benefit program to help her. Sad to say, there isn't one that fits her needs and desires.

First, I asked if Rick was a veteran. He was, having served during the years between the Korean and Vietnam wars.

"Unfortunately," I told Laura, "Rick cannot qualify for the $1,949 per month of additional income that the VA Aid and Attendance benefits could provide because he was not a "wartime veteran." Even if he could qualify, however, the VA pension is likely to be a mere drop in the bucket and would not solve Laura's monthly income/expense deficit.

We then discussed Medicaid. I explained to her that the home-based Medicaid program only covers about forty hours per week, and that is after Laura spends their assets down—in her case, to approximately $25,000. Not very much help if you consider that Laura would have to pay for the rest of the care out of her own pocket. She could take a reverse mortgage and tap into her home equity, but what would she be left with?

That's a real concern because Laura could outlive Rick by five or ten years or more. She'll need every dollar of their assets to live on since she'll lose some of their income when he dies, i.e., one Social Security check plus his pension.

This is Laura's dilemma. Put Rick in a nursing home and Medicaid will pay for his care there, but that's not what she wants. Keep him home, on the other hand, and she'll deplete their remaining assets, leaving her without enough for her own care down the road.

How did Laura end up in this predicament and what could she have done to avoid it? There are a number of things that Laura and Rick could have done to plan for the possibility of needing long-term care. But they should have taken those steps when they were both healthy. A combination of insurance, elder planning with an elder law attorney, and realistic spending with an eye toward the future would have put them in a much better position to handle the crisis they now face and given Laura many more appealing choices. It's too late for Laura and Rick, but not for future Rick and Lauras in coming years.

The Unmarried Sibling Problem

Sandra called me regarding her family. Her mom was one of ten children. Three of the siblings had never married, but lived together for many years in a home they owned together. As they reached their eighties, the siblings' health began to decline, and Sandra, as the closest family member, geographically and personally, began to wrestle with the long-term care issues that we are all facing with elderly loved ones. The unmarried siblings scenario is one we see often, with its own special set of problems.

Al, Betty, and Carl were, in many respects, like a typical married couple living under one household. They combined their income to pay many of the bills, holding a joint checking account from which they paid those expenses. They also combined much of their investments and savings in joint accounts. This included the home, which was titled in all three of their names. Everything worked out fine until Al's health deteriorated to the point where he needed nursing home care. That's when Sandra called.

Al had spent down his retirement accounts in his name alone, and some of the money in joint accounts, but when Sandra went to apply for Medicaid, they asked for five years of financial records so the caseworker could determine where all of Al's money went. And that's where she ran into a problem because, for so many years, Al, Betty, and Carl had combined much of their assets. So who's to say what was Al's, what was Betty's, and what was Carl's? Sandra thought she could just divide by three, but the caseworker questioned the transfers into and out of those accounts, suggesting that Al owned more than a third of these accounts.

Therein lies the problem we see so often. By combining their assets, the three siblings had muddied the paper trail necessary to establish that Al had spent down all his assets. Why is this so important? Because if Al is spending his money for Betty's or Carl's benefit, that is a transfer for less than fair value, and Medicaid will impose a penalty—a period of ineligibility—for benefits. This applies equally to Betty and Carl, should they need Medicaid in the future. We need to separate their assets and clearly establish that each is paying their expenses from their own assets.

We were able to help Sandra navigate through the Medicaid process and explain all transfers into and out of Al's accounts—with some difficulty. We also helped her separate Betty's and Carl's assets, so things will go a lot smoother if Betty or Carl needs nursing home care and Medicaid.

Oh, and, "What about Al's ownership interest in the home?" you may ask. There is an exception in the Medicaid rules that permits the transfer of the home to a sibling who has an equitable interest. That was no problem here since both Betty and Carl had owned and lived in the home as long as Al.

Jim's Grandmother Owes Medicaid $50,000—Now What?

I received a call last week from Jim. His tale was a variation on the same theme you have heard me reiterate throughout this book—how the Medicaid rules are a trap for the unwary. Jim's dad had cared for Jim's grandmother until he could do it no longer and placed her in a nursing home. When she ran out of money, Dad applied for and obtained Medicaid for Grandma. Everything was fine until Jim received a letter from Medicaid about a year later stating that unless the state received $50,000 in thirty days, it would kick Grandma off of Medicaid.

During the course of our conversation, Jim told me that Dad had a joint bank account with Grandma, which Dad transferred to himself about a year before he applied for Medicaid. The state apparently ran a check on Grandma's Social Security number and turned up the account. Jim didn't know for sure why it hadn't been disclosed on the original application, but to make things more complicated, Jim's dad had recently died. Jim told me he pleaded his case to the Medicaid caseworker.

"The account was always Dad's, and at some point he put Grandma's name on the account," he said. He then added, "Dad was Grandma's caregiver, and so this was simply repayment for those services and other money he paid out of his own pocket for her care."

I patiently explained to Jim that he needs to back up those statements with documentation. I asked him how much in receipts he could prove Dad spent.

"About $5,000," Jim replied.

"Well," I said, "the other $45,000 is still subject to a Medicaid penalty for being a transfer for less than fair value."

"You see," I explained, "the Medicaid system works differently than the criminal system. In the criminal system, you are innocent until proven guilty. The Medicaid system views it the other way around. If you can't prove by written documentation how you spent the money, then it will be treated as a penalty."

I could now hear the panic in Jim's voice. "The nursing home is calling us daily, demanding to know whether we are going to pay back the money," he said. "We've tried to talk to the Medicaid caseworker, to no avail. What do we do? Will the nursing home kick Grandma out?"

Jim's problem is a common one, made more complicated because Medicaid wrongly approved Grandma's application, and now wants its money back—and the one person who might have been able to provide the answers has died. And I know what you may be thinking—just because the state made a mistake in approving the application in the first instance doesn't mean they waive a right to get the money back.

I explained to Jim that he could appeal the state's decision, but the appeal process is a lengthy one, at which he must present his evidence. And given his inability to answer many questions because Dad has died, it makes Jim's case a long shot at best. In the meantime, someone has to pay the nursing home that is caring for Grandma. At a private-pay rate of $10,000 per month, the bill will quickly run up.

I asked Jim about his dad's estate.

"Dad has a house worth about $200,000," he told me. "We haven't probated his will yet, but I am the executor named in the will."

I advised Jim that negotiating with Medicaid to repay them out of Dad's estate might be the best route to go at this point. Because it will take time to sell the home, however, the state will likely want assurances that they will be repaid. And the clock is running down on Grandma's Medicaid eligibility. But the best thing for Jim and his family is to keep Grandma on Medicaid and in the facility where she has been for the last eighteen months.

There was a long pause. Jim processed what I said. He wasn't happy, but he recognized that this was his best option. Had his dad sought advice before applying for Medicaid, he would not have been left with this mess. But I also told Jim that he should consider himself lucky. At least his dad left assets with which to repay the state. Without those assets, who knows what would have happened? Jim, or some other family member, would have had to step up and pay the bill, or be comfortable walking away from the problem entirely, leaving Grandma with no one to look out for her well-being.

"But Mom Wanted Me to Have the Money"

Nora's mom has been living at home with the assistance of Nora and some private aides. Mom is now in her nineties, her health is declining, and she needs even more assistance. Nora called me because she is anticipating Mom's money running out in a few months, and Mom will probably need nursing home care.

As Nora explained, "I want to be prepared."

Nora told me that Mom is down to about $50,000 in assets. I asked about transfers, and that's when she told me that two years ago, Mom gave her a gift of $50,000. I asked if she gave her other daughter, Amy, a gift as well. Nora told me that Amy is well off and doesn't need the money, and that Mom wanted to "compensate" Nora for all the care she would be providing.

Nora acted surprised when I told her that although she thought she was planning ahead, she was actually too late and now in what we call "crisis mode." That's because Mom's gift makes her ineligible for Medicaid.

"But I've been providing care for Mom. She's really just paying me for care that if I wasn't providing, we would have to hire someone to do," Nora exclaimed.

I told her that the state doesn't look at it that way. In fact, I've had discussions with the state's attorneys in which it is clear that, philosophically, they feel that families should provide care without compensation, that it is simply a case of hiding money. In my view, that's a simplistic and unrealistic way to look at it. I see many cases where children stop working to care for aging parents. They lose income that they need to support themselves.

But it's of no help to Nora to talk about how things should be. We have to just deal with how they are. Mom could have transferred assets to her, but it had to be for fair value. In other words, Mom and Nora needed to enter into a caregiver contract in which Mom paid Nora for care that, if not provided, would have necessitated hiring an aide. And, no, Nora can't go back retroactively and sign that contract. The state presumes Mom made a gift to Nora, and that carries a Medicaid transfer penalty. I told Nora that if Mom needs care, she'll either have to give the money back or pay for Mom's care at the private-pay nursing home rate for seven months, the length of the penalty.

Nora listened and then told me that she doesn't have the money to give back. However, her sister, Amy, does have the money.

"Shouldn't she cover it since I have been taking care of Mom?" she asked.

I told her that this could possibly be a solution, but legally, Amy is under no obligation to do that.

So, where does that leave Nora? In a predicament with no great solution. But again, one that could have been avoided with proper planning.

Almost Divorced and
then Tragedy Strikes

Gloria and Ted were married forty years and raised a son together. Over the years, however, they grew apart, and when their son entered the military and his career took him overseas, they realized that there was no reason for them to stay together. They agreed that a divorce and pursuing separate lives made sense. Gloria and Ted owned a home together, but not much more in the way of assets. Ted agreed to give Gloria the home. In return, she agreed not to seek alimony. Problem solved—or so they thought—until Ted suffered severe head and neck injuries in a car accident.

Probably, twenty years ago Ted would not have survived his injuries, but advances in medical science saved his life. However, Ted remained in a coma for several weeks. After regaining consciousness, he could not speak and had limited movement of his arms and legs. He was transferred to a rehab facility, where he began intensive therapy. It is too soon to tell the extent of his recovery or if he will need to remain in a nursing facility for a lengthy period of time.

Meanwhile, Gloria now has a problem. She is still married to Ted. The nursing facility is pressing her about how she will pay for his care if he needs to remain there. Emotionally, she is torn. She and Ted have agreed to a divorce, although it's not final yet. But she also knows that Ted has no family, other than their son, but, again, he is overseas. She is also concerned about finances. She doesn't have the funds to pay for nursing care at $10,000 per month.

To make it even more complicated, Ted never signed a power of attorney. As his spouse, Gloria is looked at as Ted's decision maker, but legally, she has no right to make those decisions. Beyond that, some of the answers to the questions on the financial side of things may benefit her, but maybe not Ted. Since their intent, before the accident, was to part ways, is she even in a position to act in Ted's best interest? If he needs Medicaid, the home can be protected for Gloria as the healthy spouse. But what happens when the couple isn't really still "together"? How does that change things?

Because Medicaid treats the married couple as one unit, their assets are combined for purposes of determining Ted's eligibility. The home is an exempt asset, as long as the healthy spouse continues to live there. The solution then seems clear. Transfer Ted's interest in the home to Gloria. After all, that's what they had decided upon before Ted's tragic mishap. But hold on a minute.

Ted had agreed to give the house to Gloria because he had more earning potential. This was a way to even things up. That isn't the case anymore. He can't work, and doctors don't know if he'll ever again be able to earn a living. If not, then can he really afford to give her the entire home, leaving him with literally nothing? If he is able to leave the nursing facility, where will he go and how will he pay for it?

There is also the matter of who can make decisions for Ted. Right now, it is not clear whether he has capacity. He never executed a power of attorney, so the only option is a guardianship, but, again, who is going to be the guardian? We probably would look to the spouse first, but Gloria was about to divorce Ted. That doesn't automatically eliminate her as an option, but a court is certain to question whether she can act in his best interest. Their only child is in the military overseas, and there doesn't appear to be any other family. Maybe a court-appointed guardian is appropriate here.

So then what happens to the home? Although Gloria doesn't want to abandon Ted in time of need, she is also concerned about her future. There may be a solution. Ted can qualify for Medicaid if Gloria remains in the home, but Medicaid rules require that Ted's name be removed from the deed. That should be fine for Gloria, but someone has to protect Ted's interest.

Gloria still wants to proceed with the divorce and feels that the agreement they had should remain in place. The question then is whether Ted wants to change the agreement. He didn't consult an attorney when he and Gloria reached their agreement. He didn't think he needed one nor did he want the expense. Now that his mental capacity is questionable, however, he needs proper legal advice, especially if he must transfer his interest in the home to Gloria. Will that be permanent or just temporary? They may disagree on that.

And that's what makes this so complicated. Gloria and Ted are still interconnected in so many ways. They need to work together to reach the best result for both of them. This is not what either of them planned for, but when a medical catastrophe hits, long-term care issues will radically change anyone's life.

Better to Be
Ahead of the Curve

Last month, we lost one of our clients to an unfortunate accident. Doug was suffering from the early stages of Alzheimer's disease and living at home with his wife, Liz. Liz was twenty years younger than Doug and still working to support the couple. We had begun to long-term care plan and recommended a part-time home health aide for Doug while Liz worked.

Early one morning, while Liz was still asleep, Doug awoke to use the bathroom. The progression of the disease had recently caused Doug to become increasingly unsteady on his feet and he had experienced a few minor falls, but he was resistant to using his cane. When Liz awoke, she noticed the bathroom light on. When she went to investigate, she discovered Doug in the bathtub. He probably lost his balance, fell in the bathtub, and died from the blow to his head. The news was devastating.

Could this tragedy have been prevented? Did we, as counselors to Doug and Liz, do everything we could? Certainly, a situation like this one calls out for the use of a personal emergency response system (PERS) or medical emergency response system (MERS). (Life Alert is the one most people know.) These systems enable seniors, in the event of emergency, to contact a call center, which in turn notifies the police, ambulance, or fire services. The senior wears the device as a wrist bracelet or necklace pendant. It is impossible to say whether Doug would have had time to use it in this instance.

There is, however, a broader lesson here. When we talk with clients about planning for long-term care, especially with families that are already in crisis mode, their focus is usually on the here and now, which is certainly understandable. What services or assistance does Mom or Dad need right now? What most fail to realize, however, is that the level of need is anything but stable. What Mom or Dad needs now isn't likely to be what they need six months or a year from now. But there isn't a set schedule as to when those care needs will increase. It won't be the same for everyone. And there won't be anyone tapping you on the shoulder to say, "Now is the time to move to a safer environment."

We so often talk with families about getting the appropriate level of care. It might mean in-home care. It could be selling the home and moving to a facility. It's never easy to hear, usually frightening to consider, and often the issue of cost is a primary obstacle. The failure to adapt, however, can have serious consequences, as we saw in Doug and Liz's case. It is best to be "ahead of the curve," not waiting for something to happen and then reacting to it. Tragedies can be avoided—and financially, a better result is the outcome as well.

How to Avoid Committing Medicaid Fraud

When it comes to long-term care planning, the earlier it's done, the better off you'll be. One of the primary reasons for this is the Medicaid five-year look back. As we've been saying, Medicaid will look back through five years of your financial records to determine if you have done anything with your money that would cause you to be ineligible for benefits.

Now, you might ask, "How am I supposed to know if I violate a Medicaid rule when I don't even know what the rules are?" And that is precisely why planning well in advance is so important. Trying to go back and change what you did after the fact can get you in some real hot water. Allow me to explain.

When we meet with clients who are well on their way to needing nursing home care or are already in a nursing facility, Medicaid is starting to really come into focus for these folks. When we then look through their finances, we so often find transactions that, if carried out with an understanding of the Medicaid rules, would have put them in a much better position.

For example, I have written about the right way and wrong way to pay for aides. In the case of family members serving as home aides, typically, there is no written agreement as to the amount of compensation or the scope of the work. Without that agreement, Medicaid views the transfers as gifts subject to a Medicaid penalty. In some cases, real estate or bank accounts have been transferred, or so the family thought. Without a proper understanding of the Medicaid rules, those transfers of assets out of the senior's name actually are not transfers and, to the dismay of the family, are still subject to being spent down.

When I tell clients this, sometimes their response is, "Can we create a written agreement memorializing all the care I provided to Mom for all these years?" This typically involves "backdating" documents.

My answer is always an unequivocal, "No." Backdating documents involves creating a document, such as a deed or a caregiver contract, and then making it appear that it was written and/or signed on an earlier date.

Not only is it dishonest, it is also a federal criminal offense to falsify an application or documents in order to obtain Medicaid benefits. This is known as Medicaid fraud, and it caused an Ohio attorney to lose her license and be brought up on felony charges. In her case, she backdated a deed three years to start the clock running on the Medicaid penalty.

That's why it is so critical to understand the rules before you take a course of action. And the only way to do that is to engage in planning with a qualified professional who understands the rules and can guide you accordingly.

"I Was Just Following the Medicaid Caseworker's Instructions"

There are so many ways to get tripped up by the Medicaid system. Here's yet another one. John was agent under power of attorney for his mom who, was in a nursing facility. Over the past three years, he had spent Mom's money down for her care and then applied for Medicaid. He met with the caseworker, muddled through the process of providing all the documentation necessary, and answering all the follow-up inquiries over the next six months, and finally received approval. All sounds good. What John did—or didn't do—with Mom's income, however, is where he ran into a real problem.

Medicaid rules require that the Medicaid recipient give his/her income to the nursing facility, and Medicaid will then pay the rest up to the Medicaid reimbursement rate, that is the rate at which the state pays the nursing home. If I apply for Medicaid in January but don't receive approval until July, I must give the nursing home my income each and every month starting in January. John didn't do that. But it's his reason why that is a lesson in why you don't want to do it yourself.

Mom was living in an apartment, paying rent. When John met with the Medicaid caseworker, he says she suggested that he keep paying the rent on the apartment in case Mom wasn't accepted on Medicaid and needed to go back home. John understood that to mean that he should use Mom's Social Security income to pay the rent, which is what he did. Of course, he then didn't have that income to give to the nursing home. So, when he received word of Medicaid's approval, he thought it was smooth sailing. Except that Mom now owed the nursing home close to $15,000, her Social Security income for the past six months.

He tried to explain to the nursing home that he followed exactly what Medicaid told him to do, but the facility is demanding payment and is ready to file suit against his Mom and possibly John as the agent under the power of attorney. His mistake is in relying on the state employee to guide him. The employee either flat out gave him incorrect information, or in trying to be helpful and offering him advice outside the scope of her job, didn't make it crystal clear. In other words, although it might be a good idea to keep the apartment for a few months, the caseworker should have made it clear that payment of the rent cannot come from Mom's income, which absolutely had to go to the nursing home. Either way, he took some bad advice and ended up in a whole lot of hot water that could have easily been avoided if he had just sought out the proper guidance.

No Money, No Penalty,
No Medicaid

I received a call the other day from Margie, who was at her wits' end. Last year, her dad's Medicaid application had been denied. Dad's finances were quite simple. He had no money to his name. What little he had in savings he had spent down for his care and other needs. Dad received $1,300 per month in Social Security. He rented an apartment not too far from where Margie lived. There were no transfers from Dad's account in the last five years. Dad's health was getting progressively worse, and Margie didn't know where to turn. So, why wasn't he eligible for Medicaid?

It all sounded straightforward. But then I probed a little bit deeper. I asked Margie how Dad pays his rent, food, insurance premiums, and home assistance with only $1,300 each month.

"Well, actually," Margie told me, "I am supplementing his income."

I learned that Margie was transferring $750 every month into his account so that he would have enough to pay his bills. I asked Margie which Medicaid program she applied for. She said she wanted to keep Dad in his apartment as long as she could, so she applied for the home-based Medicaid program. That's all I needed to hear. I had the answer.

Medicaid has an income eligibility limit of $2,022 per month. If you have more than that, you can't qualify for some of the Medicaid programs, but you can for others. In Margie's case, she applied for one with a hard cap, so to speak. But Dad has $1,300 in income. Why wouldn't he be eligible?

That's because there is a specific Medicaid regulation that counts as income any regular contributions by family members over an extended period of time. And that's exactly what Margie was doing when she deposited $750 each month into Dad's checking account, giving him $2,050 of income per month, $28 over the limit. I explained to her that it would have been better for her to simply buy her Dad some of the things he needed. This way, there would be no income and he would have been well below the income cap.

The good news is that with this change, Dad can now be eligible for Medicaid. The bad news is that it took Margie a year to call us to learn this information. Dad lost a full year of benefits. Just another example of how, when it comes to Medicaid, looks are deceiving. What appeared to Margie to be so simple actually cost her tens of thousands of dollars and a lot of heartache and stress.

Danger of Acting on
the Wrong Information

If you have ever struggled through the long-term care system, you know that getting accurate information is one of the most frustrating aspects. It seems the more people you talk to, the more confusing and contradictory the process becomes. Acting on the wrong information can be costly. A call we received last week from Jim illustrates this point.

Barry's mother has kept his father in their home with aides for the past two years. But now, he is in the latter stages of Alzheimer's. Mom is overwhelmed, stressed, and concerned that money is running out. What will she live on? Barry is now assisting Mom in searching for a suitable nursing home, and hoping to qualify for Medicaid because Mom is healthy and may outlive Dad by some years. She'll need every dollar she can preserve.

Qualifying for Medicaid in the case of a married couple is complicated. Medicaid takes a snapshot of the couple's countable assets as of the first day of the first month that the applicant spouse is continuously institutionalized. That number is then divided in half, and the healthy spouse can keep one half of the assets, but not more than $109,560 (this number is adjusted each year). The couple must spend down the rest of their assets to below $2,000.

Barry reported to me that one nursing facility told him that his mom could give the facility advance payment of several months of nursing care at their private-pay rate while they are applying for Medicaid. Once the application is approved (it can take two to four months, and sometimes longer, to receive word), the facility would refund whatever amount from that deposit they don't need because Medicaid is then picking up the cost. So, for example, if they deposit $60,000 with the nursing home to cover the cost of the first six months and Medicaid says they will start paying from month four, then the home would refund $30,000. Barry said it didn't sound right to him. I told him he was absolutely correct.

What many don't realize is that the money held by the nursing home on deposit is a countable asset, so it affects both the snapshot, or starting number, and the target spend down or ending number. That money isn't part of the spend down until it is paid to the nursing facility for services received. Medicaid doesn't allow for payments in advance of services. If you "pay" the nursing home for six months, all you have done is move your asset from your bank account to the nursing home's bank account, but it is still yours.

I explained to Barry that his mom could lose many months of Medicaid benefits, which could dissipate assets she will need for her own care. He was thankful that he called us when he did. We are now preparing his dad's Medicaid application, guiding his mom through the process to insure that she will preserve what little she has left, and the nursing home will be compensated for the care they provide.

Tying Up
Loose Ends

Tying up legal loose ends is so important. Sharon and Steve were divorced fifteen years ago. They had split their assets, with Steve keeping his retirement account and Sharon keeping the house. Steve now needs nursing home care.

"It shouldn't be a problem," I told Sharon. "He'll need to spend down his assets and then qualify for Medicaid."

Then Sharon revealed her problem. Steve never legally transferred title to the home to Sharon. The deed still reads "Steve and Sharon, his wife."

This situation is actually more common than you might think. Sharon and Steve's divorce wasn't too complicated because their children were adults and they didn't have much other than the house and retirement account, which were close to equal in value. Sharon hired an attorney to "put the divorce through," and Steve represented himself. For reasons Sharon doesn't recall, Steve never signed a deed transferring ownership.

This could be a real problem for both of them. That's because unless Steve can prove he legally no longer owns the home, it could be countable and part of a required spend down toward long-term care. One of two things could happen. If the house is sold, then half of the proceeds may need to go toward his care. If the home is not sold, the state could put a lien on the home for Medicaid benefits it pays out on Steve's behalf during his lifetime.

"But didn't he give the home to Sharon in the divorce?" Well, yes, but he has to prove he received equal value back and must actually complete the transfer, which he hadn't done.

As long as Sharon (or Steve) can produce a written agreement showing the exchange of the house for the retirement account, that won't be a problem. Sharon assured me it's in writing. She just has to dig it up. I told her now would be a good time to do that. The longer she waits, the harder it may be to locate. And the state won't take her word for it—they will want the physical evidence.

She then asked me about preparing a deed. "Would we need to backdate it fifteen years?" she asked.

"Absolutely not," I told her. The signing date should never be backdated.

"Won't Medicaid treat the transfer as occurring now, making it subject to the five-year look back?"

I told Sharon that isn't an issue. As long as she can prove there was an equal exchange, it won't be subject to a Medicaid penalty and the deed signing is a formality anyway. Legally, she acquired ownership fifteen years ago. She just has to prove it.

Chapter 14

Alternatives to Nursing Home Care

Continuing Care Retirement Communities

Continuing care retirement communities (CCRCs) are communities that provide a full continuum of care for their residents. They have flexible accommodations designed to meet their residents' health and housing needs as their needs change over time, offering independent living, assisted-living, and nursing home care, usually all in one location.

As a requirement for admission to most CCRCs, residents are required to pay an entrance fee or a lump sum "buy-in," which, in addition to other things, guarantees the residents' right to live in the facility for the remainder of their lifetime. In addition to the entrance fee, residents also pay a monthly service fee.

The entrance fee is often, but not always, reimbursable (at least partially) if they move from the facility, if they pass away while a resident at the facility, or if they otherwise terminate the contract. Many contracts also contain a provision wherein an individual is able to use a portion of his entrance fee toward the monthly resident charges if the resident exhausts his resources and becomes otherwise unable to pay.

Before the new Medicaid law [the Deficit Reduction Act (DRA) of 2005], the entrance fee was generally not considered an available asset for Medicaid eligibility purposes. However, the DRA changed all that. Now, an entrance fee is considered an available or "countable" asset if: (1) the contract provides the entrance fee may be used to pay for care should the resident run out of money and become unable to pay their monthly charge; (2) the individual is eligible for a refund of any remaining entrance fee when the individual dies, leaves the community, or otherwise terminates the life care contract; and (3) the entrance fee does not give the resident an ownership interest in the CCRC.

Furthermore, under the new law, CCRCs are given the authority to include in their contracts a provision that requires residents to spend all of their resources on their care before applying for Medicaid benefits (essentially disallowing any Medicaid planning or asset protection once the contract is signed).

Basically, when an individual applies for admission to a CCRC, the application requests full disclosure of an individual's resources. Before the new law, regardless of the amount of resources an individual declared, the CCRC could not prohibit the individual from doing any long-term care planning or asset-protection planning and then applying for Medicaid. As stated above, however, CCRCs can now contractually require a resident to spend down all of their assets they declared at the time of admission before applying for medical assistance. This new provision will greatly limit the ability of CCRC residents to protect their assets once admitted to the community.

Dangers of Putting All Your Eggs
in One Long-Term Care Basket

In the past, I have written about the financial risks of investing in a continuing care retirement community (CCRC). In 2009, Erickson Retirement Communities, which operates CCRCs in ten states, filed for Chapter 11 bankruptcy, reinforcing many of the concerns I have often expressed to clients.

CCRCs are communities that provide a full continuum of care for their residents. They have flexible accommodations designed to meet their residents' health and housing needs as those needs change over time, offering independent living, assisted-living, and nursing home care, usually all in one location. As a requirement for admission, most CCRCs require residents to pay an entrance fee, or lump sum "buy-in." In Erickson's case, this can range from $150,000 to $400,000, and there lies one of the concerns.

So often I see people consider committing almost their entire savings to the entrance fee.

"The CCRC is going to provide my care no matter what level I need," they tell me. "And the entrance fee is refundable." (Which is true in Erickson's case.)

My reply, however, is that even if it is refundable, there is no guarantee you'll get it back if the company collapses financially.

Erickson is a good illustration of that. Although it did emerge from bankruptcy after restructuring its debt, if that had not happened, many people could have lost their deposit monies, which could have gone toward paying off its debt. There are no certainties in life (other than death and taxes, as the saying goes). So, you've got to have a contingency plan in the event that the CCRC can't deliver on its promise. Remember, you could be living in their community for ten to fifteen years or longer. A lot can change in that time.

It's important, therefore, not to put all your eggs in one basket. If you do invest in the CCRC model, and it certainly can be a good option for some, make sure you do your "due diligence," as we attorneys are fond of saying (i.e., do a background check on the company), and make sure you've got a backup plan. This means the company shouldn't be holding all (or substantially all) of your money. You've got to have sufficient money remaining after you've paid the entrance fee, to finance a backup plan, because without any money, you've really got no plan.

Adult Day Care

Adult day care is a wonderful alternative for families struggling with the care of an aging or disabled parent, spouse, or loved one. Adult day care centers can also provide supervision and assistance each day for a senior who is not quite ready for assisted-living or long-term care.

Each center has a staff of trained health-care professionals, including registered nurses and therapists, to help those members with complex physical or psychological problems and needs. Adult day care centers provide a structured program that includes a variety of health, social, and supportive services in a safe, protective environment.

Services are provided during daytime hours, allowing caregivers the peace of mind they need to continue working, or simply providing them with a much-needed respite so they're able to face the challenges of day-to-day caregiving.

Members of adult day care centers can look forward to a variety of challenging, interesting, and entertaining activities each day. Their caregivers can feel confident that excellent medical and therapeutic care will be provided by an experienced staff of health-care professionals. Most centers provide a light breakfast or morning snack, lunch, and an afternoon snack. Operating hours can vary, but most centers operate during standard working hours, Monday through Friday 8:00 AM to 5:00 PM. Some centers have extended hours and are open on weekends and holidays.

For those individuals who meet the requirements, Medicaid, VA, and other funded programs cover adult day care services. Long-term care insurance policies may also cover the cost of adult day care centers, so it is important to examine your policy carefully.

Respite Care

Long-term care for people suffering from Alzheimer's disease and other progressive, degenerative neurological diseases comes in many forms. Most people are familiar with nursing homes, assisted-living facilities, adult day care, and home care administered by professionals and family members. Another type of care that you may not have heard of is called respite care. This type of care is as much for the caregiver as it is for the ill family member.

For many, care is provided by family members. As anyone who has provided this level of care for any length of time knows it is an exhausting task, both mentally and physically. It is a full-time job, but not one typically limited to "nine to five." It is often a 24/7 task, and the toll, especially if the caregiver is a healthy, but elderly, spouse, can be harsh. That's why respite care is so important.

Respite care is a form of short-term relief for the primary caregiver. That caregiver may need time away to "recharge the batteries" or to address his/her own health issues. There are various programs and services available to provide care to the ill loved one while the caregiver is taking a break. This can range from home health care to adult day care to overnight care in a licensed facility, such as an assisted-living facility or nursing home. The care is temporary, usually a period of days or weeks at a time.

Financial aid for respite care may also be available through your local Alzheimer's Association's chapter. In some states, the program may provide reimbursement of up to $1,000 in respite care expenses incurred during the three-month period beginning on the date of acceptance into the program. Eligibility is not limited to people with Alzheimer's, but is open to individuals suffering from other related progressive, degenerative neurological dementia. Although funding for the Caregivers Respite Care Assistance Program is limited, it does not require disclosure of financial information. And there is no downside to applying. If funds are not available when you apply, your application will be kept on file for twelve months. For more information, go to www.alznj.org.

Chapter 15

Long-Term Care Insurance

Long-Term Care Insurance—The Basics

Long-term care (LTC) insurance, unlike most health insurance plans, pays for the cost of your care when you need permanent help with activities of daily living (dressing, bathing, toileting, walking, eating). Depending on the LTC policy, covered services may include nursing home care, at-home care, assisted-living facilities, and/or adult day care. Although some insurance plans, including Medicare and Medigap, may pay for a limited number of days in a nursing home or short-term care at home, they have no extended benefits.

A good policy can help ensure you get the care you need at a time when your health-care costs may be at their greatest. Generally, purchasing LTC insurance is a good idea for individuals who do not anticipate the financial ability to privately pay for long-term care, currently averaging about $80,000 to $100,000 per year or more in most areas of the country. Premiums are based on health, age, and type of policy. Most financial planners recommend LTC insurance be purchased in your late fifties or early sixties, when your health is still good and the cost still affordable. LTC insurance plans vary as to when and how much they will pay for long-term care expenses.

When do policies begin paying? Typically, policies establish standards that you must meet in order to initiate payment. Most will begin covering expenses when you are unable to perform a set number of activities of daily living or if you suffer a cognitive impairment, which requires substantial supervision, and when a doctor certifies specific care is necessary. It is highly likely there will be an "elimination" or "deductible" period, an initial period of time during which you are receiving care but your policy is not yet paying for benefits (this could be up to a year).

How much will your policy pay? Some policies have a daily or monthly benefit limit, which provides a predetermined amount that the policy will pay. Others have a maximum or lifetime benefit limit that provides a predetermined length of time or dollar amount that the policy will pay. Many have both a daily limit and a maximum limit.

What are the drawbacks? Other than the cost of the premiums, the most obvious drawback is that not everyone can obtain a policy. If you have a pre-existing condition, you may not find a policy for which you qualify. Or, perhaps your policy will simply exclude payment of care for your specific pre-existing condition(s).

Is long-term care insurance right for you? The decision to purchase LTC insurance is not one to be considered lightly. Although it is a great way to avoid privately paying for elder care, LTC insurance is not the solution for everyone. Not every policy will provide the coverage that best suits you. You should purchase your policy from an honest, knowledgeable professional, who not only understands LTC issues, but will find a strong policy from a reputable company that takes into account your family's health history, current financial situation, and alternative resources.

MetLife Drops Long-Term Care—
What Does It Mean for You and Me?

I have been saying it for years now. Long-term care is a growing problem in this country, one that won't go away. With the population continuing to age as 77 million baby boomers have started to turn sixty-five, no one knows whether we are prepared to handle the sheer number of people entering the long-term care system. Perhaps a recent announcement that MetLife is pulling out of the long-term care insurance market is an indication that we must pay closer attention to this growing problem.

The reasons for MetLife's decision are twofold, rising number of claims and decreasing interest rates on reinvestment income. This comes on the heels of recent announcements by John Hancock and Genworth that they are raising premiums—in John Hancock's case, by as much as 40% for individual policies. On the other hand, companies like Northwestern and New York Life have not raised rates. Rather, in some cases, new products have been introduced.

So, what conclusion can we draw from all this news? For one thing, long-term care is something that everyone ought to examine very closely, and for many who are approaching senior status, they should put the issue at the top of their list of issues to tackle. And although I do believe that long-term care insurance is an important part of the solution, a well-crafted long-term care plan shouldn't rely too heavily on any one thing. Just as diversity in investment is wise, so is diversity in planning. You can't "set it and forget it" because, as we have been witnessing, the insurance industry is still wrestling with decisions on how to make long-term care insurance "work."

MetLife says they can't make it work. There are too many claims and not enough money to cover those claims. Did MetLife mismanage their business, or is this an industry-wide problem? I am certainly not knowledgeable enough about MetLife, in particular, or the insurance industry, in general, to be able to answer that question. I certainly hope it isn't an indication of more companies pulling out of the market. More choices are better for the consumer. But what I do know is that the warning signs are there for anyone paying attention. Long-term care is the greatest threat to financial security in this country. Ignore that fact, and you do so at your own peril.

The Government's Latest Long-Term Care Solution

President Obama's health-care reform law, which Congress passed in 2010, has continued to generate much controversy and fear, including, in some cases, death threats against politicians in Washington who voted for it. I have been asked my thoughts on the long-term care provisions contained in the bill, known as the Community Living Assistance Services and Supports or, to add yet another acronym to our vocabulary, CLASS. First, let's go over the specifics as we know them.

CLASS creates a voluntary government program under which participants will pay a monthly premium, which will then guarantee them a small benefit to cover their long-term care needs. However, they must pay into the program for at least five years before claiming the benefit. The program is not supposed to be funded with any taxpayer dollars, but rather through the premiums collected from healthy participants.

Participants will pay a monthly premium through payroll deductions. The amount has yet to be determined, but reports are that it will be in the $180–$240 per month range, although it can be increased on an annual basis to insure the program is actuarially sound. The benefits are promised for life, to cover long-term care needs. The criteria have yet to be determined as far as what degree of impairment is necessary to qualify for benefits. The dollar amount of benefit has been reported to be anywhere from $50 to $75 a day.

Employers who participate in CLASS will automatically enroll their employees, although anyone can opt out of the plan. Self-employed persons and those whose employers choose not to participate will be able to join CLASS through what has been termed a government payment mechanism. Those are the basics as we know them. So, is this program going to be a savior or just another ill-conceived government program? I wouldn't hold out any hope that it will solve, or even make a dent in, the growing long-term care problem. Why?

For one thing, the specifics are very sketchy. The Department of Health and Human Services is supposed to put together regulations that will govern the administration of the program; thus, CLASS won't be rolled out for two years. Add to that the five-year pay-in requirement before you can put in a claim for benefits, which means we won't see any impact from this program until 2017. And that's if you believe that the details will all get worked out on that time schedule. (I wouldn't bet on it.)

And how about the benefit amount of $50 to $75 per day, which equates to $1,500 to $2,250 per month? Anyone who is dealing with a long-term care expense knows how little that is when compared to a minimum $4,000 assisted-living facility charge and a $10,000 nursing home charge per month in many areas of the country. For those being cared for at home, $50 won't cover much more than two to three hours of in-home care a day. That's without considering that, with inflation, the cost of care will surely be significantly more than it is now. I haven't heard anything about cost-of-living increases being included as part of this program.

I also have my doubts about the financial soundness of the program. Will there be enough people paying into the system, for enough time, to cover those collecting lifetime benefits? In other words, is the program actuarially sound, to use insurance jargon? We've seen how the Social Security system is being stretched because of an aging population, with not enough workers contributing to the system and people collecting benefits much longer than was ever anticipated. Will employees in their forties and fifties commit to a payroll deduction that will reduce their take home by $200 a month, when they are already struggling to pay their bills in recessionary times? Is this realistic, especially if there is no guarantee that the premiums won't increase on an annual basis? My experience tells me that the average person's reluctance to address long-term care needs—the "it will never happen to me" mentality—won't change. And five years doesn't seem like a long-enough time to collect money into the program before starting the pay-outs.

All in all, I don't expect much from the CLASS program. By the time it has any impact, in the best case scenario, the oldest baby boomers will be in their seventies and the already overburdened long-term care system will need more than what this program can offer.

Chapter 16

Special Needs Planning

Disabled Child Receives an Inheritance—Will He Lose Government Benefits?

Maxine calls with the following problem. Her father recently passed away and left a sum of money to each of his grandchildren, including Maxine's son, Jordan.

"So, what's the problem," you ask. Jordan is twenty-five and mentally challenged. He is disabled, doesn't work, and receives Medicaid. Maxine is concerned because she heard that receiving the inheritance will cause Jordan to lose his benefits. She's correct if his assets exceed $2,000.

"Is there anything that can be done?" she asks desperately.

The answer is to set up a special needs trust, but the timing of doing so is critical. The law has established certain safe harbor trusts that allow recipients of Medicaid and other needs-based government benefits to keep those benefits and place their assets into a trust to be used for their "special needs." These trusts, however, have very technical and specific rules surrounding their setup and administration.

For example, the trust must be irrevocable and established by a parent, grandparent, guardian, or court. The disabled individual cannot set it up himself. The trust must provide that the disabled individual is the only beneficiary and that the assets can only be used for special needs and not for food, clothing, or shelter. The trust may also need to include a "payback provision," which states that any assets left in the trust when the beneficiary dies will be used to pay back government benefits first. Oh, and the trust cannot be set up if the disabled person is over the age of sixty-five. These are just some of the many restrictions and requirements.

So, let's go back to Maxine and her problem. We can absolutely place Jordan's inheritance in a special needs trust. It probably is best to have the court act as the grantor, so we'll need to file papers. It is also important that we do this before assets are ready to be distributed from the grand-father's estate. Once the inheritance is made available to Jordan, he may lose some months of benefits before the court establishes the trust. He doesn't actually have to receive the assets for them to "be available." A typical estate can take several months or longer to administer, so while the executor is gathering estate assets and paying debts and taxes is the best time to get the trust set up.

Keep in mind that the laws in this area are very technical; therefore, it is always best to hire an elder and disability attorney who is very familiar with these types of trusts. And, where possible, it is better for the family member leaving assets to the disabled relative to set up a special needs trust in his or her will or leave the gift to a trust that already has been established by another family member. That is what we call a "third-party special needs trust," but that's a whole other discussion.

Should I Leave My Disabled Child's Inheritance to Another to Hold?

For a variety of reasons, parents often wish to distribute their estates equally among their children but not necessarily to each child outright. That may be because the child has a disability, substance-abuse problem, issues managing money, or other financial problems. Many people attempt to solve this problem by leaving that child's share to a sibling to "hold and manage" for his brother or sister. Jack's tale is a cautionary one against the dangers of employing what would seem to be an "easy" solution.

Jack's dad had recently died, leaving his estate to Jack and his two sisters in equal shares. But Dad's will actually left Jack two thirds of the assets because his sister, Lucy, has special needs. She is not capable of managing her money and would lose her government benefits if she received her inheritance outright. Jack, however, was just diagnosed with Alzheimer's disease and may need nursing home care within the next few years. He understands that he will have to pay for that care but doesn't want to use Lucy's money for his care. There's one big problem. It isn't legally Lucy's money.

You see, Dad specifically disinherited Lucy in his will. The will makes no mention of his intent to have Jack take care of his sister. It just says that Jack inherits two-thirds of the estate. Legally, it's his money, so if he needs long-term care, he'll have to spend down his money and Lucy's before he can qualify for government assistance.

What Dad should have done was set up a special needs trust in his will and left Lucy's share to that trust. He could then have named Jack as the trustee and his sister Helen as a backup trustee. Lucy would not lose her benefits. Jack would not have to spend down that money for his care. In fact, he can't, since the money is not his. And if he can no longer serve as trustee, then Helen can step up.

Could Jack set up a trust now? The answer is yes, but because Medicaid rules are quite complicated, the assets transferred to that trust would still subject him to a Medicaid transfer penalty. If Lucy was his daughter and not his sister, then he could avoid the penalty. In other words, Dad could have done it for Lucy because of the parent/child relationship.

What Jack's problem shows us is that sometimes the "easy" solution creates problems that are far more complicated to solve than the original problem. Although it's possible that Jack may still be able to protect Lucy's inheritance, it is far from certain, and much will depend on how long he stays healthy.

Index of Essay Titles in Alphabetical Order

A

A Closer Look at Reverse Mortgages 157
A Medicaid Story that Starts Out Badly but Turns Out Just Fine 43
Adult Day Care 203
Almost Divorced and then Tragedy Strikes 185
Alzheimer's Disease and Government Shutdowns 152
Assisted-Living Medicaid—The Risks of "Going It Alone" 45
Assisted-Living Resident with No Money and No Medicaid 162

B

Better to Be Ahead of the Curve 187
"But Mom Wanted Me to Have the Money" 183
"But Mom Won't Live to One Hundred—Or Will She?" 93

C

Can I Add My Children's Names to My Bank Account
    to Protect It from Medicaid? 70
Can I Be Paid to Provide Care for Mom? 64
Can I Get Medicaid if I Already Get VA Benefits? 142
Civil Unions and Medicaid 37
Continuing Care Retirement Communities 199
Crisis Planning—Nothing Left But the House 49

D

Dad Gets German Reparations Money—Does Mom Get to Keep It? 68
Dad Owns His Home and Needs Care 167
Danger of Acting on the Wrong Information 195
Dangers of an Unlicensed Home Health Aide 171
Dangers of Putting All Your Eggs in One Long-Term Care Basket 201
Declining Stock Market Leads to Long-Term Care Nightmare 164
Disabled Child Receives an Inheritance—Will He Lose
    Government Benefits? 210
Does an Inheritance Count for Medicaid? 34

E

Early-Onset Alzheimer's... 150

F

Failing to Probate in a Timely Manner... 115
Frequently Asked Questions about Medicaid.................................... 12

G

Guardianship as a Substitute for Poor Planning 130
Guilty until Proven Innocent: How the Medicaid System Differs from
    the Criminal System 20

H

Health-Care Directives—The Right to Make Medical Decisions 126
Home for the Holidays 75
Hope for Haiti: Despair for Mom? 24
How $250,000 Went up in Smoke 175
How a Call from Ann's Attorney Saved Her $90,000....................... 63
How Can the Government Tell Me I Can't Help My Family?............ 59
How Harriet's Estate Plan Destroyed Her Family........................... 118
How Home Ownership Can Be a Benefit in a Medicaid
    Spend-Down Scenario.. 55
How Long-Term Care Can Destroy an Estate Plan......................... 106
How to Avoid Committing Medicaid Fraud.................................... 189
How to Lose Medicaid 158
How to Plan for the Future 5
How to Turn a Simple Estate Matter into a Complex Mess 117
How VA Benefits Could Have Saved One Family 143
How We Saved a Family $240,000... 61

I

I Don't Have an Estate Tax Problem—Do I?................................... 111
"I Was Just Following the Medicaid Caseworker's Instructions".... 191
I'm Turning Sixty-Five—Should I Enroll in Medicare? 138
I've Got a Living Trust, So I've Got Long-Term Care Planning Covered........ 87
If Dad Needs Nursing Home Care, Will the State Take Mom's Home?............ 39
If We Apply for Medicaid, Have We Given Up?............................... 96
If We Move to a New State, Do I Need a New Will? 103
Is a Child Responsible for Not Pursuing Medicaid for a Parent?.... 160
Is Medicaid Really Biased? 8

Is My Family Business at Risk Because of Long-Term Care? 66
Is Remaining at Home Always the Best Option?.. 82
Is the Recent Change in Social Security Policy a Sign of More to Come? 6
"It's Dad's Money—He Can Do What He Wants with It, Right?".................. 165

J

Jim's Grandmother Owes Medicaid $50,000—Now What?........................... 181

L

Laura's Dilemma—Don't Let It Be Yours 177
Living Trusts... 104
Long-Term Care Insurance—How Does Medicaid View It?............................ 72
Long-Term Care Insurance—The Basics.. 205
Long-Term Care Planning—A Real-Life Picture 83

M

Married—Well Not Really.. 35
Medicaid Myths 14
Medicaid: The State's Bizarro World?.. 22
Medicaid's Disabled Child Exception... 32
Medicaid's Division of Assets—What Is It?.. 16
MetLife Drops Long-Term Care—What Does It Mean for You and Me?........ 207
Mom Needs Help but Won't Accept It—Can We Apply for Guardianship?... 132
Multigenerational Homes—A Long-Term Care Solution? Maybe.................... 85

N

New Estate Tax Law in 2011 110
NFL Seat Licenses and Medicaid—Huh? 38
No Money, No Penalty, No Medicaid.. 193

O

Obamacare—What Do Seniors Need to Know? 136
One of the Clearest Warning Signs of Dementia 148

P

Paying for Nursing Home Care 10

R

Respite Care 204

Retirement Accounts—Should I Take More than the
 Minimum Requirement Distribution? 91
Reverse Mortgages 155

S

Saving the Home 153
Should I Leave My Disabled Child's Inheritance to Another to Hold? 212
Some Married Couple Spend-Down Options to Consider 57
Spent Down? Well, Maybe Not..26
State Pension Crisis—How Will It Affect You? 95

T

The Best Kept Secret in Long-Term Care Planning 140
The Big Difference between Medicare and Medicaid 134
The Dangers of an Improperly Drafted Will 99
The Difference between Elder Law and Estate Planning 3
The Government's Latest Long-Term Care Solution 208
The Home—To Transfer or Not to Transfer 51
The Long-Term Care Perfect Storm...77
The Relationship between Gift Taxes and Medicaid...30
The Right Way and the Wrong Way to Reduce a Medicaid Penalty.................74
The Right Way and the Wrong Way to Hire a Home Health Aide 169
The Risk of Going the Medicaid Application Process Alone.............................41
The Second Marriage and How It Impacts Long-Term Care 89
The Second-Marriage Long-Term Care Problem..176
The Team Approach to Long-Term Care Planning..78
The Uncertainty of Alzheimer's Disease...146
The Unmarried Sibling Problem 179
Transfer of Home Leads to Medicaid Mess 161
Tying Up Loose Ends...197

U

Understanding Life-Sustaining Measures 128

V

VA Extended Care Benefits 145

W

We Don't Owe Any Estate Tax, So What the Heck Is Inheritance Tax? 122
What Families Need to Know Before a Crisis Hits..80

What Happens if My Bank Refuses to Honor My Power of Attorney? 124
What Happens When a Veteran Dies While a Claim is Pending? 144
What is a "Step Up in Basis" and Why Do I Want to Keep It? 53
What is the "DRA"? 18
What Michael Jackson and Yung-Ching Wang Can Teach Us All 108
What to Do When a Loved One Dies 113
When Can an Alternate Executor Take Over? 101
Why Do I Need a Will? 97
Why Edna's Estate Plan Is No Better Than Harriet's 120
Why Good Recordkeeping is so Critical to Medicaid 28
Why Long-Term Care is a Woman's Worst Nightmare 173
Why Pay Someone to File a Medicaid Application I Can Complete Myself? ... 47

Resources

The Ant and the Grasshopper, *Aesop's Fables*, Jerry Pinkney, Chronicle Books, 2000.

http://www.wikipedia.org/, Wikimedia Foundation Inc., San Francisco.

About the Author

Yale S. Hauptman, Esq.

Yale S. Hauptman is a New Jersey and New York licensed attorney, who has been focused on elder law for more than 15 years. He and his wife have a law practice in northern New Jersey. Yale has personally helped thousands of seniors and their families plan for the complicated and emotional journey through the long-term care system. He has been featured in both local and national media and has been quoted in *The Bergen Record*, *The Newark Star-Ledger*, and *Financial Advisor Magazine*, among others.

A graduate of Rutgers College and Albany Law School, Yale is a member of the Essex County Bar Association, New Jersey Bar Association, and National Academy of Elder Law Attorneys as well as his local Chamber of Commerce. He is a frequent lecturer on elder law topics to attorneys, financial professionals, and health-care professionals as well as the general public.

Yale and his wife, Laurie, have three children, who someday they may call upon to assist them in providing for their own long-term care.

For more information, please visit

www.HauptmanLaw.com and

www.BeNiceToMeBook.com